Voices from Grandview Woodland

IN CELEBRATION OF THE CITY OF VANCOUVER'S
125TH ANNIVERSARY

CREATED AND COMPILED BY
THE UNDER ONE UMBRELLA SOCIETY

© 2011 Under One Umbrella Society and named contributors. All rights reserved.

Published by Vivalogue Publishing Canada Ltd.
117 Third Avenue, New Westminster, BC V3L 1L7

Cover and book design by Magda Figueredo

Sketches and cover artwork by Bill Pope

Photos are the property of the authors unless otherwise indicated.
Additional photos were contributed by:

Donna Clark

Brian Collins

Ella Mae Lansdowne

Kelley Montgomery

Damian Murphy

Ken Paquette

The following individuals contributed to the editing of the manuscript:

Gail McDermott

Monica Dare

Denys King

Damian Murphy

Alka Murphy

ISBN 978-0-9865036-7-2

Printed and Bound in Canada

LIST OF PATRONS

The printing of this book was made possible by the financial support of the following patrons:

MICHELLE BARILE

CAROL BARTEAUX

PETER BONNY

BEVERLY CHEW

DONNA CLARK

BRIAN COLLINS

BARRY CONROY

MONICA DARE

JANE DAVIDSON

THE KETTLE FRIENDSHIP SOCIETY

MARCIA GAMBLE

CHRISTIAN GRUENIG

KATIE HUME

LIZA JIMENEZ

KAMALA & SUSHIL KALIA

LIST OF PATRONS CONT.

NANCY KEOUGH

JULIE MACLEOD

GEORGE MANDER

IAN MARCUSE

ISABELLA MORI

DAMIAN & ALKA MURPHY

BARBARA & DOMINIC MURPHY

CATHY O'CONNOR-MORRIS

KEN PAQUETTE

LINDA ROBERTS

KRISTIN ROBERTS

JAN ROBINSON

JILL SCOTT

SALLY STICKNEY

SANDRA TAYLOR

COLIN WHEATON

ACKNOWLEDGMENTS

The Under One Umbrella Society gratefully acknowledges the City of Vancouver whose grant opportunity funded much of the work that went into publishing this book. The Society also wishes to thank our community partners and story hubs who helped our outreach efforts tremendously:

Watari Youth, Family and Community Services

The Kettle Friendship Society

Britannia Community Services Centre

Peer 2 Peer

Urban Native Youth Association

Grandview Woodland Community Policing Centre

MOSAIC

Vancouver Aboriginal Transformative Justice Services Society

newSTART

Kiwassa Neighbourhood House

A special thank you to Watari, The Kettle Friendship Society and Britannia Community Services Centre for additional funding for the project and for their ongoing support and encouragement.

Thank you to all who purchased this book; you have helped contribute to the work of the Under One Umbrella Society. All proceeds from the sales of *Voices from Grandview Woodland* go directly to fund the society's Under One Umbrella Homeless Connect event. This annual day-long service fair held in the Grandview Woodland neighbourhood helps those that are homeless, at-risk of homelessness or just having a hard time in East Vancouver connect with local social service providers.

This book would not have been made possible without the tireless efforts and contagious enthusiasm of our editor and publisher Lynn Duncan of Vivalogue. Our thanks as well to Magda Figueredo for her design skills.

Final acknowledgment is reserved for those members of the community who responded to our call and contributed their stories and added their voices to this collection. This book is by you and it is for you.

Thank you.

FOREWORD

The Under One Umbrella Society is a proud recipient of a Vancouver 125 grant, and pleased to present Voices from Grandview Woodland as our contribution to the city's 125th anniversary. The anthology of stories from Grandview Woodland residents past and present capture some of the rich history of this East Vancouver neighbourhood and give voice to the people who live, or have lived, here over the last 125 years. But this land's history begins much earlier.

The neighbourhood now known as Grandview, or Grandview Woodland, or even Grandview Woodlands as some call it, remains part of the territory of the Coast Salish peoples whose descendants long lived on this land for many, many generations before the European settlers arrived. In acknowledging this territory we honour the people who first called this place home. May we never forget the full history of where we stand today.

In fact it is the aboriginal tradition of storytelling as a means to preserve histories and teach future generations that originally inspired this project. The stories you will read and voices you will hear in this collection are freely shared for your contemplation. The story criteria for contributors were left completely open with but two main conditions - the stories had to be true and they had to be short.

The Under One Umbrella Society is a grassroots volunteer community group made up of workers and residents of the Grandview Woodland neighbourhood. The Society has been working together on social justice issues like poverty, homelessness and harm reduction in the neighbourhood since 2004. In this time Under One Umbrella has shaped an extensive network of community allies and partners. This collection of stories, like much of the work we do, would not have been possible working on our own.

The first step of the project was to establish ten story hubs in the community; places where people interested in the project could get more information about the project or help with their stories. The story hubs are listed in the acknowledgement and the histories of their work in the community form part of this book.

The journey to complete this project continued through the summer of 2011 with members of the Society doing outreach in the community at public events, festivals and by reaching out to everyone up and down Commercial Drive, the main artery of this vibrant neighbourhood.

Story contributors to this anthology range in age from four to 98 years old and, in our opinion, represent a truly diverse cross-section of those people who call this neighbourhood home. But the stories do not end here. One of the greatest revelations of compiling this book has been the realization that it could take a lifetime to capture all the incredible stories of the people who live here. This book is by no means complete but certainly does do justice to our goal of recording for now and the future Voices from Grandview Woodland.

TABLE OF CONTENTS

Some Irish Pioneers in the Early History of Grandview	Bruce Macdonald	1
Britannia Community Services Centre		4
Independence	Carol Snider	5
On the Edge of Nature	Hannah Govorchin	6
Evelyn Harris – One of Commercial Drive's Characters	Bruce Macdonald	8
New Pizzeria Uncovers Old Crust	Kevin Potvin	11
My Life in the Tough East End	Sally Stickney	13
Shoot Out at First and Commercial	Jak King	16
In the Driver's Seat	Jean Russell	18
Everybody Loved Charlie Russell	Jean Russell	20
Circle of Love	Jean Russell	22
Down Memory Lane	Rose Brisky	24
Odlum Drive Childhood	Penny Lim	26
Peer2Peer		27
A Lifetime on the Drive	Mary Bosze	28
At Home in Little Italy	Linda Massaro	30
Magnet Home Hardware	James Buonassisi	32
Pennies from Heaven	Bea Beaulieu	34
Magic Envelopes	Monica Dare	35
Raising Families on McSpadden	Divina Soriano Leacock	36
Roll Out the Barrel	Eileen Mosca	38
Joe's Café	Bruce Macdonald	39
La Quena	Linda Forsythe	43
Disability, This Ability	Kagan Goh	46
Messengers of Hope	Nancy Knickerbocker	48
L'il Albert	Barry Conroy	49
Macdonald School	Barb Parrott	50
Kiwassa Neighbourhood House		52
Just One Block in Grandview	Bruce Macdonald & Gail McDermott	54
Wall Street Community Garden	Jan Robinson	57
Our Grandview Woodland House	Penny Street	58
The Garden the Community Loved	Ian Marcuse	62
Home	Marcia Gamble	65
Commercial Health Centre	Aaron Goldbeck	66
A Yogi on the Drive	Carol Barteaux	68
Vancouver Aboriginal Transformative Justice Services Society		70
Two Weeks on The Drive	Melanie Konkin	71
1582 William Street	Adrienne Foster	72

Remembrance Day	Linda Roberts	73
The Card	Alka Murphy	74
Only on Commercial Drive	Sandra Taylor	75
GW Community Policing Centre		76
Coffee To Go	Mary Smith	77
Urban Native Youth Association		78
Sorry Mister, You Have to Move	Damian Murphy	80
Wild and Free	Francis	83
Waiting for the Sun: The Awakening	Troy Pugsley	84
An Everlasting Camping Trip	Richard Nuisker	86
And I Was Sorry Too	Connor Murphy	88
We Are All Characters; Life Too	Sook King	89
PeaceMeal at Trout Lake	Lingling Maranan-Claver	90
Neighbourhood Book Exchange	Seth Makinson	92
MOSAIC		93
And My Laundry Does Too	Laura Blake	94
No Sheep Allowed	Amber Flea	95
Welcome to the Neighbourhood	Brian Collins	96
The Epic of Elvis	Elvis	96
The Kettle Friendship Society		97
The Before Story	Carl	98
My New Family	Larissa	99
A Little Bit of Me	Dustin	100
Ten Years Later	Jayleen (Sweetheart)	101
Experience, Strength and Hope	Audrey	102
You and Me	Cherryse Kaiser	104
newSTART		105
A Crop of Kindness	Anika King	106
Playing Guitar	Amanda Lucas	108
Commercial Drive	James	108
Rhythm of the Drive	Kelley Montgomery	109
Quantum Physics	David Berger	112
A Place of Acceptance	Teresa Diewert	114
How I See the World	Teresa Diewert	115
Noah's Memorial	Teresa Diewert	118
Stranger in the City	Joan	121
Watari		122
Glen Caponero and the Black Dog	Peter Worthington	124

Some Irish Pioneers – IN THE EARLY HISTORY OF GRANDVIEW

Colonel McSpadden

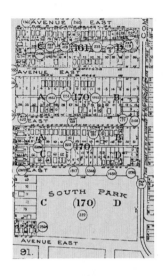

E.J. Clark's Park in 1910

Forbes Vernon

A **number** of persons of Irish heritage played notable roles in the earliest days of Grandview in the 1880s and 1890s. All three Irish Grandview pioneers described here are linked to the naming of Grandview's streets. Street names were some of the things that first appeared in the uninhabited, logged-over forestland.

You could say modern Grandview began when a real estate developer of Irish heritage, Ephraim J. Clark, donated some land for a park near the city limits in 1889. It became the second park in Vancouver after Stanley Park. It was called South Park, long before Trey Parker and Matt Stone (whose father is Irish) thought of the animated TV series.

Little else happened until other real estate developers completed an interurban railway from Vancouver to New Westminster in 1891. This being the time before the automobile, these developers knew that the best way to sell real estate at the outer edge of town was by providing access by streetcar.

In 'Grandview' there still were no roads or houses, just Vancouver's first neighbourhood park site. Things really didn't get going until the first streets were roughed out in 1902 and water lines reached the neighbourhood in 1904. By then the first long north-south street in Grandview had appeared and was given an Irish name, Clark Drive, after Mr. E.J. Clark.

Eventually a road was built along the edge of the streetcar line. It was named 'Park Drive' after the only thing along its route – South Park at its far end, at Vancouver's southern border at 15th Avenue. In the pioneer years many of the roads built through vacant land were named after their apparent destination. After 1905 businesses began to line Park Drive. The new business people realized a name change was in order. To clarify the new purpose of the road, Park Drive was changed to Commercial Drive in 1911. At the same time South Park was renamed Clark Park.

Meanwhile, in 1904 Irishman George McSpadden built the first substantial home in northern Grandview, on a whole city block he owned. Later he sold the block to the government and it became the other park right on Commercial Drive, Grandview Park. During the Great War 1914-1918 Colonel McSpadden formed the 11th Regiment Irish Fusiliers, basing it in Grandview Park. McSpadden Street and McSpadden Park, by Commercial Drive between Fourth and Fifth Avenue, are named after him. He was the city's first Building Inspector, and he was Grandview's alderman for most of 1907-1913, the period when Grandview was built out.

Grandview's main route to and from Vancouver's downtown has always been Venables Street. The origin of this Irish street name involves more real estate stories and a trip to Ireland.

In the 1990s I worked on the book *Street Names of Vancouver* for its author, Elizabeth Walker. I can report that many landowners in Vancouver named city streets themselves, after themselves. This happened naturally because when owners subdivided their acreage into small lots and streets, they were usually free to name the streets.

The earliest Vancouver landowners typically purchased a 160-acre district lot for about $1 per acre. In hindsight this was a great deal — about 10 cents for an average-sized city lot!

As real estate was taken up in the original city, comprising Gastown, the West End and the East End (now Strathcona), the land by the northwest corner of Grandview came into play. Its owner was Forbes Vernon, who was born in Ireland.

Forbes Vernon came to BC from Ireland to become one of the first non-natives to settle in the north Okanagan Valley. Here he established the first orchard. It later grew into one of the largest producers of fruit in the British Empire. The new town of Vernon was named after Mr. Vernon in 1887. In 1891 he sold his 13,000-acre ranch to Lord Aberdeen, the Governor General of Canada from 1893 to 1898.

Elites and other insiders such as Vernon, an MLA, did very well buying cheap wilderness land on remote Burrard Inlet just before it skyrocketed in value after Vancouver was established in 1886. The first cross-Canada railway arrived in 1887. Just 25 years later the land at the centre of downtown Vancouver, formerly one dollar an acre, was selling at a rate as high as two million dollars per acre.

'Forbes George Vernon' got to name the streets on his 65 acres by northwest Grandview. In the north he named 'Forbes' Street as the first east-west street, and in the south he named 'George' Street as the first north-south street. He named 'Vernon' Drive as the main north-south street, running down the middle of the northern part of his land, and he named 'Venables' Street as the main east-west street across the middle of his land. Why 'Venables'? I was able to solve this mystery with a stroll through the history of Ireland.

Twelve hundred years ago Ireland had no towns, but consisted of a rural countryside covered with poor peasant farms, interspersed with dozens of relatively wealthy Catholic monasteries. In their search for plunder, Vikings (Scandinavian pirates) discovered Ireland in 895 AD. They made regular successful pillaging raids throughout the undefended island, looting the monasteries of their treasure and livestock as well as taking people for slaves. The Vikings got more organized and established permanent bases along the Irish coast. These bases for raiding also served as trading centres for their newly acquired slaves and stolen goods. The Viking plunder centres developed into Ireland's first true towns: Dublin (841 AD), Cork (846 AD), Waterford (850 AD) and Limerick (922 AD).

The Viking Age in Ireland is considered to have ended in 1014 when High King Brian Boru organized an army and emerged victorious over the Vikings at Clontarf near their first and last stronghold, Dublin. Clontarf Castle was constructed here in 1174, and it soon became a base of the Knights Templar.

Clontarf Castle, childhood home of Forbes George Vernon

In 1649, after the English invasion of Ireland under Oliver Cromwell, the title to Clontarf Castle ended up in the hands of John Vernon, Cromwell's Quartermaster General. Clontarf Castle then became the ancestral home of the Vernon family for over 300 years.

Forbes Vernon was born and raised in the famous Clontarf Castle, the son of John Venables Vernon. Mr. Venables Vernon built a huge new Clontarf Castle in 1837, just in time for his son Forbes' birth in 1843.

Such rich history surely adds to the reasons for a son to name a street after his father.

Recently the new Clontarf Castle has been converted into a spectacular 111-room Dublin hotel. Only two blocks away is Dublin's Vernon Avenue, and the Clontarf Distillery that makes Clontarf 1014 Irish Whiskey.

Meanwhile in Vancouver, Forbes Street is gone, but George Street is one-half block west of Vernon's key intersection of Venables Street and Vernon Drive. One-half block west of George Street is another castle, the landmark La Casa Gelato at 1033 Venables Street. This 'castle' has been an ice cream store since 1983, and it is currently the home of 518 flavours of ice cream, of which there are 218 flavours available for ice cream cones at any one time.

I would like to propose that owner Vince Misceo make room for a new flavour on his menu, Irish, but nevertheless homegrown in Grandview: *Venables Vernon Ice Cream*

It would have a Clontarf 1014 Irish Whiskey flavour, with highlights of Okanagan apple. Cheers!

Britannia Community Services Centre

Britannia Community Services Centre Society has its origin in cooperative community action in the 1970s. Local citizens and various civic agencies created the organization in 1974 to coordinate and integrate a wide range of human services to meet the interests and needs of residents.

Through a locally elected Board of Management, the non-profit society provides a leadership role in developing and facilitating educational, recreational, library and social services for the communities of Grandview Woodland and Strathcona. In collaboration with personnel from the Vancouver School Board, the Vancouver Public Library Board and the Vancouver Board of Parks and Recreation, the Society manages the approximately 18-acre complex which includes, but is not limited to, the following facilities: 4 gymnasiums (A, B, C & D), 5 tennis courts, a soccer field, a running track, a softball field and several outdoor basketball hoops. Britannia Preschool and Britannia Out of School Care are located here on the Britannia site. There is a 5-8 room in the Preschool at Grandview Park and a separate Pre-Teen room near the Library. Our 25-meter pool is equipped with a 1-meter diving board, a rope swing and a children's slide. There are dry saunas in the change rooms and a well-equipped fitness gym upstairs. We provide access to all members of our community, including persons with mobility issues. There are also numerous off-site programs and activities.

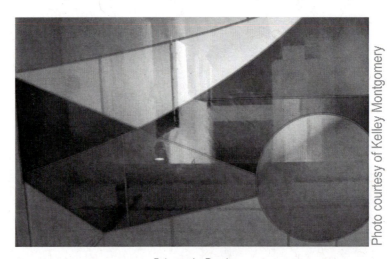

Britannia Pool

Photo courtesy of Kelley Montgomery

Independence

When I was growing up at 805 East Pender Street, kids had a lot more independence than they do today. There were a lot more opportunities for adventures in daily life.

When I attended Seymour School the big trick, at lunchtime, was to race home before the train came by and made us late for lunch at home (those were the days when we had one hour for lunch). Sometimes the older boys on my block would waylay me and not let me pass in time to beat the train. I met one of them later on in High School at John Oliver and he just laughed at his childish prank.

Another adventure was helping the local newspaper boy deliver the Vancouver Sun. He made me go inside the apartment building to deliver there. At seven years of age and in grade two I must have been very gullible and brave. Of course, this was strictly volunteer on my part.

Once I had started learning to read I figured that I didn't need to give the grocery list to the store-keeper any more. I read it out myself. My mom couldn't figure out why there were so many items that she hadn't requested.

Of course, all that independence could also have a downside. There was a BIG SEARCH on for my little sister one time. We scoured the neighbourhood and couldn't find her. She was across the street, inside the Ukrainian Hall watching a concert.

GRANDVIEW WOODLAND IS AWESOME BECAUSE…

...we're best friends but we can hold hands while walking down the street. You can do this on The Drive.
     (Penny and Christine)

On the Edge of Nature

My name is Hannah Govorchin, I am 82 years of age. I was born in Windsor, Ontario, in the year 1929, my ethnic background is Yugoslavian. When I was five years of age, in 1934, my parents drove my brother and me from Ontario to Vancouver, BC. At the time there was still existing the economic depression and welfare was given only after living in Vancouver for a year, so in order to make a living my father caught crabs, cooked and sold them. This was considered illegal and he was charged.

Our family first lived for a short while in the Vernon apartment on Hastings and Vernon Street in Vancouver. Then we moved to a three-roomed little house at 918 Raymur Avenue, Vancouver, situated at Raymur and Venables Streets. My father was a fisherman. Our neighbours were Scottish, English, and Russian. In the neighbourhood lived mostly Yugoslavs, Italians, Lithuanians and Ukrainians. I remember there were railroad tracks not far behind our house and when the old steam railway train whistle howled, it seemed to shake our house, and each night it lulled me off to sleep. The street where we lived was, I think uniquely, a one-sided short street with no houses across the street. Kids would refer to us as living at 'the dumps' but I felt I was close to nature.

The Flats stretched from our street across acres of flat land, across to where the Maple Leaf factory was far in the distance and where my little brother would wander. As well, across from our house and just in front of The Flats was a bog with frogs. Every evening they sounded like an awesome chorus. At the bog grew bulrushes and a distance away yellow broom bushes, pussy willow bushes, salmon berry bushes, wild strawberries, wild bleeding heart flowers and tall grass. At dusk time I was frightened when flocks of bats would fly about. Our house was situated well back and in front was the yard with a narrow walkway and tall grass on either side where garden snakes would frighten me.

Those were the days when we were avid listeners of the radio, used a wooden kitchen stove, our house heated with a coal furnace, and we used a roller type of wash machine. Our milk was delivered by a team of horses. I would often roller-skate on the adjacent Venables Street. I walked a few miles every week to pay five cents to go to a movie at the York Theatre. From the time we were young children, my brother and I often went to Grandview Park at Commercial Drive, playing and swimming in the pool. From where I lived, I walked for miles to attend the former Vancouver Museum and Vancouver Public Library situated at Main and Hastings Street, now called the Carnegie Centre.

I lived at 918 Raymur Avenue until I was 12 years of age. Then our family moved to a house situated at McGill and Kaslo Streets. I attended Seymour Elementary School and, several years ago, I attended its 100th anniversary. I went to Templeton Junior High School, where my three children also attended years later, and Grandview High School of Commerce, which was situated at First and

Commercial. It is gone forever as it was torn down some years ago and replaced with stores and a food market. I miss not seeing this high school and recently celebrated the high school reunion. A few blocks away I attended the Croatian Educational Home, a centre close by at Campbell Avenue and Georgia where I belonged to the Tamburica orchestra, this musical instrument being similar to a mandolin. After World War II, about 1947, the Centre was replaced with the Russian People's Home, and nearby was also the Ukrainian Hall which I attended. There used to be the Crystal Dairy situated on Commercial and First Avenue and on Victory Day of World War II, when I was 16 years of age, that day I served ice cream to happy customers. The Hammond Mattress Factory used to be situated several blocks eastward from our home.

I have three children and two grandchildren and I presently live in the Hastings East area. There have been many changes in the neighbourhood with factories, Britannia Centre, bakeries, gelato ice cream parlour, book store, pet store, cafes, market stores, etc. York Movie Theatre later became a drama theatre, and now is an ethnic movie theatre. The Flats are now replaced by Strathcona Park. Years later our house at 918 Raymur Avenue and neighbouring houses became replaced with the General Paint Factory and now every time I pass by it reminds me of my younger days.

HANNAH GOVORCHIN

Photo courtesy of Kelley Montgomery

Evelyn Harris – ONE OF COMMERCIAL DRIVE'S CHARACTERS

Evelyn Harris was a character, a unique individual who lived in the same old house at the top of William Street for 84 years. As the founding member of the Evelyn Event and the proud owner of Grandview's first recognized heritage home, she was featured in many newspaper articles and media spots through the 1990s. This was when she was in her 80s, the period I knew her.

A young Evelyn, in character

She always reminded me of a very happy and self-satisfied 12 year old girl, in part because she was the size of a 12 year old girl. She was barely 4 foot 8, weighed about 90 pounds and was very light on her feet. She had a ready smile and a real bounce in her step. She liked to claim she had the oldest intact heritage house in Vancouver. She would say she never married because she couldn't bear to move out of the house. The house still had its original kitchen, including an ornate cast iron wood stove. It is located at 1210 Lakewood, which is just past Rose Street at the end of the 2000 block of William Street. The house was formally recognized in 1989 as an A category heritage building with a Vancouver Heritage Award, the first in Grandview.

Because of the 1919 flu epidemic that eventually took a total of 50,000 lives in Canada, Evelyn's parents Viola and Harford moved the family to Commercial Drive from Edmonton that year. They first lived temporarily in the BC Block at 990 Commercial Drive, on the northeast corner with Napier Street. Today this old 1910 bay-windowed two-storey building with apartments on the second floor looks very much like it did in 1919.

In his 1990 book, *Vanishing Vancouver*, painter and historian Michael Kluckner featured Evelyn's house and he did a watercolour painting of her stove. Evelyn was proud her father kept a diary listing the purchase price of everything in the house. As Kluckner points out, in 1919 the Harris's paid $105 for the cast iron stove and $3,125 for the house.

I first met Evelyn about 1992, introduced by a neighbour who knew of my interest in history and heritage. One thing about people like Evelyn, who have lived a long time in the same place, they can make interesting local associations to things you bring up.

Evelyn's chair in the dinning room, and her stove

I had researched the history of our house at 1749 William, and found the first owner was William Jordan. He lived there from 1910 to 1934 and was the first captain of Vancouver's Fire Hall No. 5. Next to the front door we had a framed picture of Captain Jordan, badge #4, in his uniform.

The first time Evelyn came to our house, she looked at the picture of Captain Jordan in the lobby and said, "The last time I stood here was in 1920, when I came to visit my boyfriend Bobby Jordan to give him a birthday card — and here it is!" She then handed me the lovely 1920 birthday card with her child's signature.

Evelyn made a point of collecting historians. I believe the first was Michael Kluckner, with his *Vancouver: The Way It Was* (1988), and *Vanishing Vancouver* (1990, being updated and reprinted in 2012). Then Robin Ward, with his sketches of heritage buildings, *Robin Ward's Vancouver* (1990). There were others. I got included in Evelyn's collection of historians by virtue of my having written Vancouver: A Visual History (1992), and so every year she invited me to tea at her house on my birthday.

I had occasion to really appreciate the depth of her knowledge when I was hired by novelist Cynthia Flood to answer questions about some very specific details about living in Vancouver in the old days. There were about 10 questions I could not answer, so I took them to Evelyn. The first was, "How much would a party dress for a little girl cost in 1952?" She immediately answered, "They cost $2.50 — that's how much my Mother paid for one in 1952." I was astonished when she answered every question in this manner.

She was very proud of the dark-stained varnished wood throughout her house, the unaltered appearance of the rooms and their contents, and of her regular routines. Once a week she would get down on her hands and knees and clean her living room carpet by hand with vinegar and water, one square foot at a time. She would draw the living room curtains late every afternoon so the sunlight from the west wouldn't fade the finish of her antique desk. She loved sewing and had made most of her clothes. When she woke in the morning she would say to herself, "Something good is going to happen to me today!" It always amazed me how it never bothered her in any way that so many things on Commercial Drive, not to mention in the entire world, were constantly changing, not always in a good way.

She certainly got around and went out most days by bus. She would explain to you that she always wore her white gloves, and that was why she never got a cold. She always tried to sit on the side seats so that no one could sit behind her and cough or sneeze on her.

She was proud of the fact three different suitors had proposed marriage to her, but she was even happier to tell you she had turned them all down. Then she would lean over to gleefully share a final private secret, "I'm the oldest virgin in Vancouver!"

Evelyn was so self-satisfied, at age 80 she actually started an Evelyn club. Her 'Evelyn Event' consisted of women she knew and liked who had the name Evelyn. Even in her late 80s she would arrange to have lunch with her group every month, with up to 30 or 40 Evelyns attending. They would meet at Uncle Willy's on West Broadway. Occasionally she would have to inform an Evelyn that just because she had the name Evelyn didn't necessarily mean she could be a permanent member of her club. The Evelyn Event was featured on CBC radio and in the

Vancouver Courier. She also appeared in various media to show off her house.

Evelyn always expected to live as long as her mother, who died at 96 years being nursed at home in the living room by Evelyn. Sadly when she was only 88 years old, Evelyn was taken to the hospital by her doctor and passed away soon after.

As the writer of heritage plaques for the city of Vancouver, I was requested to write one for Evelyn's house just after she died in 2002. This plaque was for her participation in a program to determine authentic heritage colours to assist people in repainting heritage houses in their original old colours. Here is what I wrote:

HARRIS HOUSE
Builder: Storer J. Wing

Of eight Edwardian Classic Frame houses built here, only this 1909 house has remained unaltered. In 1919 the Harris family bought it, and for over 84 years Evelyn Harris lived here and endeavoured to keep this exceptional house in its original condition. As part of the True Colours program, the house has been repainted in the original colours chosen in 1920 by Evelyn's parents, Harford and Viola Harris. The main part of the house is Harris Brown, the trims are Harris Cream, and the lower level is Harris Grey.

One of Bruce's birthday visits to Evelyn's place

New Pizzeria Uncovers Old Crust

When workers peeled off the grey stucco covering the south wall of 1190 Victoria Drive at Napier, they glimpsed an intriguing advertisement painted on the original exterior. The ages-old sign reads 'Shelly's 4X Bakery Products,' and features a rotund and happy baker donning his baker's hat. The sign advertised a product line carried by the Victoria Grocery Store, opened by a Russian immigrant named Wilhelm Poponovich in 1926. The store remained at this location through many owners into the 1990s before an art gallery was opened- with the old letters rearranged to read first 'Dry Vigorate,' then 'Dr. Vigari,' a business since moved to Commercial Drive.

The building was originally constructed in 1922 and the bottom commercial floor was first occupied by the short-lived Globe Staty Co. Shelly's Bakery Products was established in 1910 at Ash St. and 10th Ave in Mount Pleasant by William Curtis Shelly. He was born in 1878 in Jordan Ontario and started baking in nearby St Catherine's in 1898. By 1923, Shelly's Bakery went on to establish branch plants in New Westminster, Nanaimo, Victoria and eventually Saskatchewan. William renamed the Shelly Bakery the Canadian Bakery Co in 1929 so the sign on the side of the building must date to the period between 1926 and 1929.

On his successful business credentials, Shelly ran for and was elected an alderman in 1920. In 1928 he ran for the Tories in provincial elections and won again, being named, on account of his baking background, Minister of Industry in the new Tolmie government. He went on to become Minister of Finance in the 1930s- not likely an enviable posting.

Shelly also launched the Grouse Mountain Highway and Scenic Resort in 1926 and was instrumental in laying Mountain Highway up to the ski and hiking area where he

Photo courtesy of Ken Paquette

owned 1,800 acres. He planned a major hotel before an earlier Second Narrows Bridge was destroyed in an accident and the onset of the Great Depression killed the idea. It all reverted to the District of North Vancouver for the non-payment of $20,000 in taxes.

Retired from the baking business and politics by the late 1930s, Mr. Shelly took an interest in magic shows. During the Second World War, he performed 115 magic shows for armed forces' audiences. In October of 1946 he was introduced to a gathering of the Point Grey Kiwanis Club at the age of 68 as the "foremost amateur magician in North America." The baker, finance minister, resort developer and magician immortalized on the side of 1190 Victoria passed away in 1951 at the age of 73.

The "4" in the advertisement refers to the number of round stone millings the wheat had been subjected to. Each milling removed more gum, bran and germ from the flour, and consequently made it whiter- in the age before bleaching made everything whiter. Bran and germ more quickly turned rancid and therefore dark, so it was always deemed better to buy whiter bread, reported A. Linton Davidson in the April 1942 edition of the National Health Review. He went on to add that wheat is not native to North American soil and climates, but was "introduced accidentally to the Western Hemisphere in the 16th century through admixture with rice in a parcel brought by an African slave from Spain."

Editor's Note: Reprinted with permission from the *Grandview Sniveller*, third Friday, August 2011 edition. Word is the new owner has responded to neighbours' concerns and has now preserved the nearly 90 year old sign in place.

My Life in the Tough East End

My name is Sally Stickney, but I wasn't always Sally Stickney, I had a few other names. I am 75 years old and I was born in my Grandma Edith's and Grandpa Tom Williams' house. He built that house at 2226 Oxford Street around 1915. He was originally from Hobart, Tasmania. My mom and her two sisters were all born in that house and she was the youngest. It was quite a lovely home on a double lot. My grandfather worked for the City of Vancouver in the Streets Department, when they had wooden sidewalks.

I was born August 4th 1936, at home in that house and my mother, Vera May Stock, had 96 hours of hard labour, starting around August 2nd. Dr. Walsh dropped by every four or five hours to check on the progress of my mother. He lived here on Templeton Drive between Eton Street and McGill Street, in a beautiful mansion made of brick. It was the only hoity-toity house in the whole neighbourhood. My mom only had one baby, and I was finally born naturally. The Doctor delivered me at six o'clock in the morning on August 4th 1936. When he delivered me he said to my mother, you have a beautiful little girl. My mother said "I don't want her, flush her in the toilet!" She didn't want me from the time she conceived. My mother hated me all her life, it's the God's truth. She said "I don't want her, take her away, do away with her, flush her in the toilet." I was very tiny, I was five pounds and something; it was a very difficult birth. I did have a kind of Attention Deficit Disorder problem all my life.

I wasn't born Sally Stickney. My grandpa and grandma who built that house, their name was Williams. My other grandma and grandpa were Vander-Stock. I was born Sally Marie Vander-Stock, that's Belgian. All of her children changed their names one by one to Stock. I think she had nine children.

When I was going to Hastings School, I was Sally Stock. At school in grade six I did very poorly academically but did very well in sports, volleyball, softball and grass hockey. My mother and I decided I would repeat grade six. It was very hard because all my friends went to Templeton Junior High for grades seven, eight and nine. When I repeated, I did very well. I wasn't slow or handicapped. They have a handle on it today, they call it A.D.D.

My dad worked as a longshoreman and a grain liner. My mother worked part-time at the Fishermen's Co-op at Commissioner Street, she was a fish filleter. She made pretty good money, but she didn't work too much because it interrupted her beer drinking. She also worked for the Hudson Bay Company in the 1940s when my dad went into the Army. She worked in the basement in the cafeteria and she was like a short order cook, cooking fish and chips, hamburgers and whatever. She made fairly nice money but they spent it all at the Princeton Hotel. They paid for half of the Princeton Hotel. My dad and mom would get off work and meet at the hotel, and by the time they staggered up the hill, they were pissed. I had to feed the chickens, collect the eggs and bring up sawdust from the basement to burn in the stove to cook my own egg for supper.

My other grandparents, my dad's mom and dad - her name was Melanie and his name was John Vander-Stock. He was deaf and he did nothing but pick up scrap metal and whatever in a wheelbarrow. My grandma had a bootlegging joint with girls and used to drink tumblers of straight gin. That's where my mother met my father. She was very beautiful you know, and very promiscuous. She was sleeping with two or three of the brothers - Albert, Emil (which is Mickey my dad) and Andre, who years later turned out to be gay. My mom was sleeping with the three brothers when she was 18 to 19 years old. She was drinking like a fish then. That was at my grandma's bootlegging joint on Powell and Salsbury Streets. She was very attractive, sexy, very promiscuous and loved men. That continued all of her life.

My Grandmother Vander-Stock was a bootlegger all her life and made lots of money! She had all the policemen and all the mailmen there socializing. My grandmother sold booze and girls and said "that's mother nature, if George wants to go bed upstairs with Betty, that's their business." It was money, that's how she made money. Uncle Albert would never admit it to anyone.

Emil (Mickey) was the only one to step up and marry my mom. My mom and dad lived in one room when they got married in January and I was born in August. They lived in a scruffy, scrubby rooming-house at 2167 Dundas Street. I don't even think they had a sink; they had a little hot plate. They spent most of the time at my grandfather's place on Oxford Street.

When I was fifteen, my mom and dad split up and sold the house on Oxford Street. It was a beautiful home and sold for $5,000 to five Italian families and paid off the mortgage. Both my parents were out kookying around. I think my dad found somebody, more than my mom. My mom wasn't too fussy.

To escape all this turmoil, I kind of took a shine to this guy. My mother knew his mother; his name was Kenneth Robert Brown. I married Ken at age 17. He worked at Canadian Fish, up the coast at Goose Bay, Rivers Inlet. I left home, went up there and worked one sockeye season. Before I was 18, I was divorced. He spent all of his time drinking and sleeping with all the girls at camp. Anyway, I took the Union Steamship and came home, because I was so fed up with him drinking and up all night, partying with all the whatever.

Then I met the football player, Paul Janick; he was a Marine Engineer. I met him at a bowling alley on Clark Drive and Hastings called the Palladium. He was absolutely beautiful and had a brand new Meteor car. He had blond curly hair and was very sexy looking; as it turns out he wasn't sexy at all. I fell for him and he was a big show person. I met him when I was 18 and married him when I was 21. We lived at 357 North Garden Drive; we were married for eight years.

Then Paul decided he was in love with my best friend Carlene. That one particular night I got home one hour early from night school. When I went in, all I could see was a big lady's bare bum in my bed! I never said a word; just drove to my Auntie's house and fainted on the floor. I immediately left Paul.

Herbert Ganel Stickney came into my life 11 years later. In 1974 a big gang of friends got together at Herb's Army and Navy Club. We started to date in September and we got married in December. We moved to 54th Street and Victoria in a small house.

He was a lovely man, probably the nicest person I ever met. I still miss him today. After he died I moved back to Grandview Woodland just up from where I was born. I love the East End and they will have to move me out on a gurney.

Shoot Out at First & Commercial

Commercial Drive was revelling in postwar prosperity during the spring of 1949, and no doubt it was that very prosperity that drew Robert Harrison to the corner of First & Commercial on 8th April. Harrison, a short stocky man with a round face and high cheekbones, well-dressed in a tan topcoat over a leather jacket and a sports shirt, stood outside the Commerce Bank building after parking his car just around the corner on First Avenue. It was 10:30 on a sunny morning and Commercial Drive's sidewalks were already crowded.

Harrison, who had stolen $6,000 in an armed robbery of a bank on Victoria Drive just two months previously, used a sticking plaster to attach a white handkerchief across the bottom half of his face. He then pulled a Canadian Army-issue 9mm pistol from his pocket and strode into the bank, following behind an older woman. Once inside, Harrison roughly pushed the customer aside and started shooting wildly, firing six times. Mrs. Gloria Groome, a customer, felt a bullet "whiz past her head." Others weren't so lucky. Bank manager Charles Scanlon was grazed in the thigh, while another of the bandit's bullets passed through an office door and hit accountant Arthur Pearson in the shoulder, damaging his lung. Harrison took his time stuffing $3,000 in mixed bills into his pockets and then ran back to the door.

By this time, everyone out on the street knew a robbery was in progress and an alert Fraser Transfer truck driver had blocked off Commercial to the south with his vehicle. After being alerted by a Mrs. Clarke who rushed into his shop, E.L. Williams called the police from his dry goods store on the southeast corner of the intersection while his clerk could see people standing with their hands up through the bank windows.

A cashier who had been returning to the bank from her morning tea break but had been stopped by the noise inside ran in a panic into the Quality Shoe Store next to the bank. Thirty-nine year old manager William Bishop and his father Arthur had already heard the gunfire next door. Now, William ran out into the street to flag down Constable Cecil Paul, who he knew was on motorcycle patrol. Looking back, Bishop saw Harrison leaving the bank, gun in hand, and the gunman immediately saw him. Bishop just managed to duck behind a parked car as a bullet crashed through the side of the engine hood and came out under the fender, a few inches from where Bishop crouched.

Harrison shouted "Stand back!" to the world in general and moved toward the corner where his car was parked.

A number of elderly women happened to be gathered on the corner and at least one of them attacked him with an umbrella. Harrison, realizing that his car had been blocked by the Transfer truck, grabbed one of the women to use as a shield and began to cross Commercial heading west. But the woman proved too awkward to carry and he dropped her. Just at that moment, five year old Ian Erlandson, not understanding the danger, ran by and was grabbed by the gunman to use as a shield instead.

By this time, 26-year old Constable Paul, a veteran of six years active service, had arrived on the scene and dropped his motorcycle. He pulled out his gun and deliberately fired a shot over Harrison's head. Harrison fired back, almost hitting 26-year old housewife Gloria Groome who was standing on the west side of the street. Constable Paul aimed again and his second shot hit Harrison in the forehead, killing him instantly. Blood spattered everywhere as Harrison crumpled to the ground, the boy still in his arms. The gunman's Browning automatic still had five live rounds, and 32 more rounds were later found in his pocket.

Young Erlandson was unhurt and scampered off, to be found later playing with friends near his home on Cotton Drive, seemingly unfazed by his adventure. The coolness and bravery of Constable Paul was recognized by all and he would eventually be awarded the King's Gallantry Medal. In the meanwhile, the Grandview Chamber of Commerce immediately decided to present him with a watch as a token of their appreciation. Manager Scanlon, though not badly injured, took three months' stress leave, not returning to work until July. The seriously wounded Arthur Pearson also recovered, thankfully.

In the Driver's Seat

I was born in Vernon in 1913. I went to school in Lincolnshire England for a bit and then we moved back to Vernon. Then I ran away and got married when I was 19 because my mother wouldn't let me put a lock on my bedroom door to keep my little sister Norma out. She was eight years younger than me and she and her friends used to try on my clothes after school. But they weren't smart. Instead of hanging them back up again they'd throw them under the bed and that made me kind of upset. But my mother was a snip and she said, "They'll be no locks in this house." So I ran away and married this chap from Kamloops.

This was before the war and everybody was poor but we never went on welfare. I spent that first winter in Kamloops chopping wood. Everybody had stoves in those days so we went out to the woods and chopped wood and went door to door selling it. When everything started to go, gold came on and my husband went to work in the mines. I spent a long time up at Braelorne and Pioneer Mine. Then he got to be the superintendent of big construction jobs and I used to help him. He made such big money. We built a big mill between Nelson and Trail and the airport in Pat Bay near Victoria. We also spent a winter in Alberta doing construction on the airport in Vulcan. Of course I had to do a lot of driving living in these places. When we were in Alberta there was a man who had a garage service and he had a big building like a hangar which was heated because it's pretty tough there in the winter time. Everybody who had a car kept it in there and paid monthly rent. Naturally, my car was in there because I was the boss's wife.

We stayed together 12 years and then we parted. I was not a night person and he never came home if there was a light on anywhere. I'm a different type of person. I go to bed early and I get up early. I don't stay in bed. I get up every morning before 6 o'clock even now and I'm almost 100 years old.

When I first came to Vancouver, I lived at Fifth and Lakewood. That was during the war and women had to work too. I worked parking cars at the medical building downtown, right across from the Hotel Vancouver. There used to be a place where people dropped off their cars and we had to drive them up.

After I got married again I still did most of the driving. My husband Charlie often used to work until midnight before we headed for home to Vernon for Christmas. I would be driving over the Hope Princeton highway and he'd be in the back trying to get some sleep. One time I was breaking ground through the snow because there had been no one ahead of me. Someone was following right behind me and his headlights were blinding me all the time. I hit a piece of ice and went round and round three times and threw Charlie right out of the back seat. Charlie told me I could really drive a car because we could easily have been in the ditch. But I hung onto her.

After Charlie bought himself a plane he figured he hadn't spent much money on me so he bought me a brand new Chrysler New Yorker, all leathered-up. It had everything, all red leather inside. It was just beautiful. I drove it all over Mexico and everybody thought we were rich. We weren't rich; we were just poor people from Grandview.

JEAN RUSSELL

GRANDVIEW WOODLAND IS AWESOME BECAUSE…

…it's an old neighbourhood which hasn't really changed in 100 years. It still has a mixed group of nationalities. I've lived here off and on for 30 years. Mostly, it's no stress – everybody is pretty well laid-back and easy-going. There are free dinners from churches, the Salvation Army and the chili wagon not to mention the Under One Umbrella Homeless Connect event.
   (Laurent)

Charlie Russell

Everybody Loved

Charlie was in the services overseas. He ran into me and just took a fancy. I was a big girl you know - 5 foot 5 and about 200 lbs. Lots of women then drank and he didn't like all that. I didn't drink or smoke.

Charlie wanted to go to university, and the government would have paid for it, but he also wanted to start a business and make money. We looked all over because it was hard to get places in those days. We even went up to the interior and we didn't get a place up there either. But when we came back we got this place at 2084 Commercial, Café de Soleil as it is now. After we moved here we got our cabinet making business going. We opened in 1947 and it was so busy we had two men in here. Charlie really had a big business going here. It was a great time, everybody around went up.

We rented this place when we first got it. An old Russian owned it. He didn't want his monthly payment sent to where he lived. He used to come and get it and I always gave him some hot soup. One day he came and said, "I'm going to sell and I'd like to make sure that Charlie gets it." We all loved him and hated to see him go but he sold to Charlie. Everybody liked Charlie. I don't remember the price but he charged 4% interest. I looked after the money and I got that piece paid for in two years.

Then the old lady who lived next door took a shine to Charlie. She said, "I'm going to sell my house. Would you like it?" I can't remember what we paid for it but houses weren't expensive then. We paid for it in the next two years and I've never had a mortgage since. It was going to be our home because we were right close to the business and near everything. We had it all re-plastered on the ground floor and I had such a big living room and dining room. I had a new kitchen because that was Charlie's business. We fixed the house up and had nice new things but it still had a rotten smell and we couldn't stand it. We rented it out for a couple of years. The people were nice enough but she went running into the shop to bother Charlie for every little thing. One time, it was a wasp in the basement she couldn't get rid of. Charlie was so mad he said, "I can't stand that woman. We've got to get rid of her." So we sold the house and Charlie built this all here. After that, Charlie and I were only separated twice. When he went out the door he was at work and we he came back for lunch he was home.

Once we got things going, we were loaded. The first spare money we had Charlie spent on me. The first thing he bought me was a washer and dryer for $600. That was way back in 1957. The next thing he said was, "Do we have any money?" I said, "Of course, look how busy we've been." He asked if I would mind if he learned to fly. Charlie had wanted to fly when he joined the services but they wouldn't train him because he wore glasses. So he learned to fly in Richmond. He got his license all right and the next thing he said was, "Do we have any money?" I said, "Of course." So he went out a bought a plane and paid cash for it. That's how good our business was. I learned to fly too and Charlie was very disappointed that I didn't go for my license. What stopped me was a horrible accident that happened to another pilot. A lot of people were killed and every time I went to the airport for weeks after I would see their cars still left there.

Charlie kept the plane 11 years and I always called it "the blonde" because it was so expensive. At first, we arranged a hangar in Richmond. Then they got all the small planes out of there and he had to go out to Abbotsford. He used to have to drive out there one hour, get the airplane out of the big hangar, pushing other peoples' planes aside because he was only a weekend flier, and then he'd have to come home. By this time we were not spending the winter here. We got a motor home and went away every winter.

We never had children but we had three little Chihuahuas. One was Sammy. He lived until he was nearly 20 years old and he went everywhere in that airplane. Charlie just loved him. One was Snooky, who never left my side. He was supposed to be a Chihuahua but he grew too big. We took him back to where we got him and they said there was something wrong. They offered to put him to sleep and give us a new pup from the next litter. Charlie said, "Like fun you will. That's our dog."

The third dog was Kiddo. We bought him from someone on the west side when we went to pick out a Chihuahua for my mother. There was this other little dog there that was full grown but they had become too attached to her to ship her anywhere. This dog was jumping around Charlie's legs and he asked if they would sell her without discussing it with me at all. The lady wanted $75 for him. He pulled it out of his pocket and bought her right then.

Anything that anybody needed, they just went to Charlie. He and I were on all the committees about the neighbourhood and Britannia. Those were the days when all the kids had little wagons. They'd bring 'em to Charlie and he'd fix them all up. Everybody loved Charlie Russell.

Circle Of Love

My theory is that there is a circle of love - if you give your love out you'll always get it back again. I did 40 years of volunteer work for all kinds of things. My husband Charlie and I were on all the committees about building the Britannia Community Centre and I was the president of the lounge there. We made a mistake planning it though because we put the pool table in the lounge area. The men all thought they could come in to play pool any time they wanted even though there was supposed to be a schedule. I didn't make the rules but I was there dishing them out and they used to call me 'fat ass'. One day I guess I went home looking a little funny and Charlie offered to go down and beat them up for me.

The Kettle was right across the street on Fourth Avenue then and the people from the Kettle were welcome at Britannia. They used to come into my lounge. I had one boy, a nice young man, who always used to pee outside. I used to go outside to visit and say, "Come in, I've got a nice bathroom for you, everything's in there. Don't do this out here." I was outside with him quite a few times trying to get him inside the house. Every Thursday morning I donated my services to the kitchen in the school cafeteria and we served a hot meal to all the people from the Kettle. Nancy, another one of the volunteers, did the roast, mostly at home before she came. I made hot biscuits and we all did the vegetables. Then we all ate together.

I also did a lot of work for seniors. One of the things I worked very hard on was getting portable steps put on buses. Older people couldn't get on buses because there was a big step up from the cement sidewalk. I couldn't either because of my arthritis. One day I was trying to take a bus and I couldn't get up the step and told the bus driver he would have to give me a hand. He was pleasant enough but kind of funny. When I asked where the step was, he said, "Those darn things! They're a nuisance so we hide them." When I told him I was the one who got them put on the buses, the man nearly passed out because he'd made such a noise about the whole thing.

We had the same problem when they did the centre at Trout Lake. They put a bus over there but the only way to get in it was up some stairs. I was one of the volunteers there but I wasn't one of the bosses. The leader, Mrs. Smith, and I got a walkway from Victoria Drive. Everybody uses it and you walk right into the place now.

I was also responsible for getting the steps in the pool at Britannia when they re-did it. Charlie gave $1,000 and Mr. Diamond from Hastings Park, who was always very generous, gave a big bunch of money to help. My name was put on a plaque there and Mr. Diamond and I were the ones who cut the ribbon when they opened it up again.

I went before city council a few times to get all these things done. That's when Harcourt was the mayor. One time I went in there and there was a whole long list of people scheduled to speak. The woman in charge of the list had an assistant who was a real snip. She asked me what I was doing there and I told her my name was on the list. She said, "It can't be. We don't have people like you here." People from here didn't look very special then; we look a little better now. She asked me how I could do that and I told her I could do all things through Christ. She almost had a fit. But I'm a Christian woman and I do practice my faith.

We were never people to drink and run around. We didn't go night-clubbing and tearing around. We paid our bills and paid cash for everything and shared what we had. For 13 years, until Charlie died, we gave all the interest on our money away to help feed people downtown. We did it three times a year, Thanksgiving, Christmas and Easter.

After I had my stroke and my arthritis got worse, Charlie said, "I think 40 years is long enough." I got a medal from the government for 40 years for community service. I also got a silver bowl from the City of Vancouver. It was made in Birks and had my name all on it. Only six people in the whole city received one and I was the only one who wasn't a university graduate. I was just a little thing from Grandview Woodland.

JEAN RUSSELL

Photo courtesy of Damian Murphy

Down Memory Lane

My name is Rose Brisky and I was born in 1934 at the Vancouver General Hospital of Yugoslavian parentage. We lived in Vancouver's East End at 432 Campbell Avenue, in the second house on a block consisting of small identical houses.

I have three sisters, Alice, Mary, and Katie, and I am the youngest. Mary taught me to read at the age of five. I had my own library card from the Carnegie Library at Main and Hastings.

In 1940, my father bought a large ramshackle house on three large lots with many fruit trees, a vegetable garden, and a hen house ruled by a nasty rooster who terrified me. The job of egg collecting fell to Katie who feared no man or beast.

The York Theatre was only a block away and showed a weekly serial featuring '*Nioka of the Jungle*' who was routinely captured by various African warrior tribes and who routinely escaped captivity and the tortures awaiting her by using her superior wit to avoid being decapitated. Of course, you had to wait until next Saturday to know how. Me and my gang emulated our heroine by dressing in jungle garb – courtesy of mother's old dress – and swung from tree to tree in our yard. If you could do the jungle call – see Tarzan's yodel – it was added to the fun. A tribal hut was essential, so we used slabs of wood destined for the furnace to erect a structure of some kind. But you had to know the secret password to obtain entrance. It only lasted for a short time as my father demolished it when he returned from work, shaking his head at his children's stupidity. It was a little wobbly, I admit.

Our next task was to build a victory garden to help the war effort and which was to be examined by a panel of judges. After a while we lost interest as pulling weeds wasn't much fun. We were told it was unacceptable by the panel, so Hitler could breathe a sigh of relief from this source anyway.

We discovered the Grandview Theatre had a side entrance which wasn't locked, so one of the boys would pay for admission and he would sneak us in when the theatre went dark. After the movie, we pooled our finances and ordered a milkshake at Hazel's Café next door which we passed around, each taking one delicious sip, until it was all gone.

Memories of the Grandview Woodland area – where I knew the names of our neighbours and would bring pieces of surplus salmon supplied by my father and received gifts of tomatoes and other vegetables in return – going to the fish & chip store every Friday and bringing home supper wrapped in newspaper – waiting for the milkman to come by so we could pat his horse – the arrival of our first telephone which my Mother refused to use for many years – walking to Templeton High School unafraid and unaccompanied – attending Grandview School of Commerce for one year prior to its close.

You ask when someone was kind in the Grandview Woodland area and the difference it made to one's life. It was a much kinder time without the violent drug dealers and users of today, few homeless people as there were ample boarding houses with rooms which could be paid for by relief cheques, and many churches supplied food for the hungry when asked. Murders rarely occurred – I personally don't remember any reported unlike today which is almost a daily occurrence.

What effect did this create for me – simple – a happy childhood with little fear of the dangers facing children today with drugs, drive-by shootings, kidnapping, and other violence throughout the world. Yes, it was a great time – we had no computers to play with; we played with each other not a machine; we used our imagination instead of programmed information. And we never locked our door – quite different from today sadly. So, I look back on that time and treasure my memories.

Childhood

Odlum Drive

Ah, Odlum Drive Grocery store played a main role. As a small girl, I became friends with one of the two girls of the Japanase family who owned the corner grocery. The family invited me to lunch; I recall using chopsticks different from our Chinese ones, whereas my mother asked how Japanese rice tasted. Some time afterwards, Odlum Drive Grocery changed hands to Dave and his Chinese family. Because the store lay between the No. 22 bus on Clark Drive and Britannia High School, students frequented Dave's store. Added moments of excitement!

No tall buildings. Odlum Drive Grocery a mystery to me as it had two storeys. What was up there in those apartments?

My favourite memory though belongs to the Dairyland wagon horse who galvanized the neighbourhood children. At a glimpse of its appearance, we focused our attention and energy by running up to the wagon unloading products to Odlum Drive Grocery. We wanted to pet the horse or feed it grass! Even if the wagon ambled off before we reached the store, we would chase after the wagon holding grass in our little hands. A horse - elegant, so tall and appealing. In awe, because we were little.

Nostalgia. Fresh fish on the doorstep. Shoulder pole, basket of fish on each end, an elderly Chinese man sold fish going door to door. This brings back another memory. Chickens, that is. Order a chicken from Chinatown and it would be delivered to your home. Additional types of deliveries? Cords of red cedar wood and sawdust.

Naturally, Grandview Theatre on The Drive offered cowboy heroes on Saturday afternoons. Who was playing this Saturday? Either Roy Rogers or Gene Autry. Naughty boys not deterred by the manager threatening to stop the film due to rowdiness. Some threw popcorn boxes upon the stage as he spoke.

Years later, as more mature theatre goers, we awaited the first Elvis Presley movie, 'Love Me Tender.' The price: 15 cents. We cried at the end.

Ah, the street car along Venables to downtown and up to The Drive. I recall a pharmacy on The Drive. Best of all, I remember a house arriving on a flatbed truck and landing across the street from our house. Enchanting to a little child.

Peer2Peer

Photo courtesy of Ella Mae Lansdowne

Peer 2 Peer is a team that consists of current or former addicts who want to give back to the community. We have been serving the Grandview Woodland community for approximately 15 years. The group was started by a group of people with addictions who saw their community had serious issues concerning the harm caused by drug use. These issues included used needles and garbage from paraphernalia on the ground, addicts sharing needles and increasing the risk of spreading disease, and people with addictions who did not want to deal with traditional outreach.

So what the founders of Peer 2 Peer did was start to gather together at Grandview Park in order to discuss the problem. What they came up with was that they would not wait for anyone else to fix the problem. They decided that a principle of harm reduction was preferable to the official line of abstinence and enforcement. They thought an underlying reason for the troubles in the area was that people who used drugs might be concerned that needle exchange and health care services were set up to identify drug users to the authorities. So, if that were the case, if an outreach team made up of people with addictions were to be the ones to act as liaisons between the health care services and people with addictions on the street perhaps some of the harm associated with drug use in the area would be lessened.

So weekly meetings continued to happen at Grandview Park and the group started to do outreach in the area. At that time needle exchanges were on a one-for-one basis so the outreach team would collect needles from users and off the street and exchange them one for one at the exchange. They would also distribute clean needles to people who wished them as the outreach team passed. Soon, they were known within the community and would be stopped by those with used needles and who needed clean ones.

About seven years ago, Peer 2 Peer began to be funded by the Vancouver Coastal Health (VCH). This meant that the meetings would take place in a VCH building and that the group would be supplied by VCH and they wouldn't have to go to the needle exchange. Now they would be a needle exchange. This also meant that Peer 2 Peer would be coordinated by an employee of VCH who would be the liaison between the group and VCH. This relationship has blossomed and continues to this day. Peer 2 Peer remains committed to the Grandview Woodland area and hopes to continue its work for the good of the community.

A Lifetime on the Drive

I have lived a lifetime near 'The Drive' in Vancouver East, namely the Grandview Woodland area. My father built this home where I live in 1939 and there is a fourth generation residing here with me now. This address is approximately 15 minutes from First Avenue and Commercial, when in the 1940s I attended the Grandview High School of Commerce situated at that corner. The school was torn down in the early 1950s and replaced with businesses.

A large number of European immigrants arrived in Vancouver in the 1950s and so many of the Italians settled in the Vancouver East region from downtown east to Boundary Road. They became homeowners where they raised families and introduced the new 'culture' in their way of life - the tomato plants, grape vines and bean stalks in the back yard garden and bocce in the local parks. They also changed the face of housing because they brought their skills in the art of stone masonry which was applied in their unique designs. Many occupied the businesses along Commercial Drive where they brought the barber shop, shoemaker, tailor and bulk foods such as cheese, pasta and olives. Commercial Drive in those days became known as 'Little Italy.' The name has almost faded away since many of the older businesses have closed down or moved away leaving fewer Italian ventures alive. Commercial Drive has developed into one of the most prominent areas of diverse ethnic food in the city.

My first job was on Commercial Drive at Woolworth's located between Graveley Street and First Avenue across the street from my high school. As students we worked on Friday evening and Saturdays and were given the opportunity to work the school holidays at Easter and Christmas. During the summer time, we were able to find employment at local canneries around the city. In particular, I worked at the Bestovall Cannery situated beneath the First Avenue and Clark Drive viaduct. We cleaned vegetables, packed fruit into cans, and were able to learn and participate in the process of canning from beginning to end.

After graduation, joining the work force, getting married, followed by years of raising children, I fell heavily into volunteering in schools and community in addition to working part-time on Commercial Drive for my brother, who was a notary. I became a member of a Neighbourhood Improvement Program (N.I.P.) through a Parent-Teacher Committee. This group became responsible for spending $2.5 million granted to our neighbourhood by the Federal government where we made community decisions about where and how we would spend this money. This led me to seats on other councils and groups such as the Grandview Woodland Area Council and Planning Committee and the Area Services Team to find valuable information from them about the needs for specific projects or programs in the immediate area. It was a difficult time trying to divide the money between groups but it also became a lot of fun over the years. Most of it was eventually spent on improvement in the parks, playgrounds, co-op housing, street lighting, beautification of business areas and many other enhancements. This planning committee worked closely for seven years to finalize the eventual outcome.

At the time that I was a member of the Grandview Woodland Planning Committee, we discovered a large section of the community that was the most underdeveloped area according to zoning from City Hall. This region was the section from Commercial Drive west to Clark Drive. This became a 'hot' spot for developers to jump in and start the rebuilding process quickly. Suddenly the community became a political battleground for landlords, real estate marketers, and the rental market as well. It can be seen today as a very well developed area with large apartment blocks, some co-op housing, seniors' and family housing.

As the years passed by I was approached by the local Health Department to open a Family Place for young mothers with small children who had no extended family here. I left the office to become a full time coordinator of East Side Family Place on the 900 block of Commercial Drive in the late 70s. 'The Drive' became the hub of non-profit services which included Britannia Services Centre, MOSAIC, Reach Health Clinic, Kettle Friendship Society and East Side Family Place which still exist after 35 years in the area. These agencies have remained here and expanded significantly in numbers of people they service to date. The Vancouver East Cultural Centre (The Cultch) also had its beginnings at this time with small grants for improvements and expansion.

By making improvements to its building and promoting the theatre throughout the entertainment world, The Cultch has made a remarkable name for itself in our community and the city during the past 38 years.

I retired from all employment and got involved in the seniors' arena when I became a member of the Mayor's Advisory Committee for Seniors for 15 years. This group contributed a great deal of advice and service to City Council which included such objectives as housing, health, transportation and advocacy.

The area around First and Commercial has been the centre of my life in one way or another for the past 70 years. I have seen it change a lot and I was involved in many of those changes. I am extremely grateful to this community for honouring me in many ways for my contribution to volunteering, fundraising, promoting advocacy, and serving on specific boards. There never seems to be an end to their generosity and I say "Thank you."

Photo courtesy of Brian Collins

At Home in Little Italy

I was married when I was 15 ½ years old and had my first child before my 17th birthday. My husband, my two daughters, Iolanda and Margaret, and I arrived in Canada from Abruzzo, Italy on February 22, 1966 in the middle of a snowstorm. The city looked like something out of a fairy tale but I was not charmed. If I could have, I would have gone back right away. When we first arrived we stayed with my husband's sister and her family on Bruce Street. We had one more daughter, Sonia, soon after we got to Canada.

I started work in Canada after I had only been here one week, without speaking one word of English, at a clothing factory called James Chambers. I did all kinds of sewing, including hems and buttonholes, and after a few years I went to work in Gastown in the cutting room of a leather factory.

I was always attracted to Commercial Drive because everyone spoke Italian. There were lots of Italian restaurants, bars, and stores. They used to call it 'Little Italy.' I used to go there and that's why I bought the Coast Cleaners dry cleaning shop in the 1970s (from a French couple who were old and sold it to me). It was where Il Mercato is now. I also did dressmaking there. It was around that time, in 1979, that I bought the house at 1521 Salsbury Drive (between Graveley and Grant). My name is still there, drawn in the cement near the gate.

I sold Coast Cleaners when we moved back to Italy briefly. When we returned in the 1980s I started to work at the Margaret Rose Fashion Boutique at 1744 Commercial Drive. After that, I worked at Jennifer Fashions at Hastings and Nanaimo. I also worked at home, sewing clothes for women — dresses, jackets, blouses, skirts, and suits. We had some customers who came all the way from Campbell River but most of them came from the neighbourhood. I always told them the truth and treated them well and they came to trust me. After nine years everyone knew me. I didn't always know their names so I called everyone signora.

In 1989, my husband and I separated and I bought my own apartment at Commercial and Georgia. In 1992, I stopped working and started to look after my granddaughter Erika. I volunteered at Queen Victoria School while she was a student there, until she was in grade six. When she switched over to Britannia Elementary, I switched to Britannia, too. Years later, in about 2000, my other two grandchildren, Fabbiana and Allessio, also attended Britannia Elementary. Now they live in Abruzzo, Italy and Allessio is in university in Milano.

At Britannia, I started volunteering with Rosanna at the Family Activity Room at Britannia Centre — doing cooking, crafts, crocheting, scrapbooks, and assembling Christmas boxes for single parents. In the meantime, I met Anne Jackson, the 55+ Coordinator at Britannia. I was attracted to the place because she was so kind to me. I used to walk right past the 'Seniors Centre' at Britannia because I felt I was too young for them! So then I started to go there.

I took four computer classes for seniors. Then I met Carolyn Innes at Lion's Den and I started volunteering there and also teaching scrapbooking and knitting. We started to cook special Italian dinners at both Britannia and Lion's Den.

I've also volunteered at the Vancouver Health Department in Il Mercato, and then later (2006–2007) at the Community Policing Centre on Commercial Drive, at Broadway Church in their Kidstreet program, at the Italian Cultural Centre's 'Villa Carita, and, in 2007, teaching scrapbooking to seniors at Frog Hollow Neighbourhood House.

Recently Ian Marcuse, the food security coordinator at Britannia, made a video of me and the kids in the teen centre cooking my specialty, spaghetti alla carbonara. He made a second video with Maria Buono and me making pasta with meatballs for the high school kids at Britannia. Both these videos are on Youtube!

Now I volunteer at the Lion's Den adult day care and I'm also involved with their caregivers group. We have potlucks at Lion's Den and at Britannia's 55+ every month. I am on the Britannia Seniors Committee and the Lion's Den Recreation Committee and I participate in many community events.

It makes me feel good to help people and I love Grandview Woodland. I feel fantastic because of my friends, my kids, my grandkids, and this community. Now one of my daughters wants me to sell my apartment so that we can go in together on a bigger place in Burnaby. But I've told her that I will die if I leave Commercial Drive.

GRANDVIEW WOODLAND IS AWESOME BECAUSE...

...it is very, very diverse. People are nice to me every day because is such a great place. I especially enjoy the annual Peer 2 Peer Barbeque at Trout Lake. Who wouldn't love Grandview Woodland?
(Chris)

Magnet Home Hardware

As a kid in Grandview I spent weekends and summers at the Magnet Home Hardware on Commercial Drive. At the time I thought I should be off doing stuff that other kids seemed to be having fun doing rather than counting nails and cutting keys. However in retrospect it offered some interesting memories that I'm glad to have.

The store has been in our family for nearly 50 years and has served some amazing characters, both famous and fantastic. Harry Rankin and James Barber were just two of our notable regular customers. Harry told me about the merits of DYI as opposed to hiring trades people. He strongly professed that if you pay someone to do the work, that 2/3 of the overall costs will pay for the labour. I sold a bocce ball set to Sara McLaughlin, and I sold rope to my friend Daniel, a promising photographer who later used that rope to hang himself in Strathcona Park.

And there were some who were less well-known but equally as interesting: There was one guy that came in who had the exact same beard and haircut as a Klingon from the original Star Trek series, and another whom we called Cosmic Dan – I'm sure you can imagine why.

Vittorino and Alberto were among some of the personalities who livened the experience. Vic has one of the most amazing gardens I've ever seen, and it got that way because each day he would collect old fruit and vegetables from Norman's Fruit and Salad and use them for compost. Vic insisted that each day he would walk to the bank to make the daily deposit with my uncle as his 'security', and he showed up like clockwork at 5:15. Alberto always talked about playing accordion while making the motions with his hands and yelling out "ahh – la musica". He had one of those incredible handlebar moustaches to add to the experience.

Photo courtesy of Damian Murphy

One of our regular customers was Mrs. McCluskey, who lived on Rose Street. She would, in her rough Scottish brogue, ask if I would come over to her house to change a light bulb for her. I delivered many bags of dirt and other things to her home. This year she unfortunately passed away, and as an adult in my professional role as a real estate agent I've been back in her home to help sell it.

I remember a Friday night when three guys wanted to fight my brother-in-law Ed and my dad because their car was towed from the store's parking lot while there were drinking in the pub across the street. Luckily there happened to be a police officer walking by and the crisis was avoided. In truth, it was the other guys who would have been getting a lickin' – anyone who knows the area knows that you don't park in the store's parking lot and then go off to do other business! This kind of grit was just one of those things that made the Drive 'The Drive'.

The Italian Festival left an impression on me. The Commercial Drive BIA at the time hosted the Festival and much of it was paid for from the sales of beer in the beer gardens. This made for interesting situations such as the time a guy decided to strip naked and run through the street after Italy had won the World Cup.

What has always intrigued me about the area I now call home is the interesting and strange mix of grit and toughness, simple acceptance of each others' differences, and the sincerity of the hard-working people who raised their families and built a life here. It wasn't really grand, but it was true and I've come back to raise my kids here too.

JAMES BUONASSISI

Photo courtesy of Damian Murphy

Pennies from Heaven

I moved to the neighbourhood in 1966 when my son David was three. I got a job at The Glen, which was an annex of the Napier Care Home. The Glen was sort of an overflow for people who were really sick. There were also a lot of Alzheimer's and dementia patients although we didn't know to call it that then. There wasn't enough room at the General Hospital so people would go there until they passed away. I was an Assistant Cook earning $2.19 per hour which was decent money in those days.

I found a local babysitter for David in a house down the street where the ice rink is now. I used to take him there at 6 o'clock in the morning. The babysitter would put him in bed and then go back to sleep herself. One day, one of my co-workers told me my son was walking up the lane and, sure enough, there he was – in his pyjamas and carrying his blanket. I decided I wasn't going to pay for babysitting if he was determined to follow me so I started bringing him to work. He sat all day with one of the elderly ladies there and she would keep him occupied They seemed to get along just fine. The doctor there, Dr. Brumwell, used to come in once a week. He got attached to David too. He used to sit and play with him in the office and even brought in his gerbils. David loved the gerbils and would put his head right into the cage.

The old lady had a one gallon pickle jar she used to save her pennies in. When she died, she left those pennies to David. I protested to the family but they insisted that she had left specific instructions in her will. That was a lot of money for a little boy and a lot of rolling for his mother.

BEA BEAULIEU

DID YOU KNOW...

The Kettle Friendship Society was once located in the 900 block Commercial Drive where Attic Treasures is now. The building was heated with a pot-bellied stove and an old bath-tub served as a filing cabinet. In those days, only about 10 people a day came in. Now over 100 people a day receive service and the Society has over 1,000 members.

Magic Envelopes

I was born in New York but moved to Vancouver in 1974, and I lived in various areas including the West End and my houseboat in Ladner. In 1984 I had to move back to New York to take care of my father who had been diagnosed with cancer. While in New York I lived in Park Slope which was a very ethnically and culturally diverse neighbourhood. When I returned to Vancouver in 1988 I was looking for an equally diverse community, and Commercial Drive in Grandview Woodland was certainly all of that and more. I was lucky enough to find an apartment that I could afford and I moved in.

While in New York I had fallen victim to a financial scam that by 1989 had stripped me of everything I owned. I found myself in very dire financial straits, completely depressed and unable to work, and on social assistance for the first time in my life. My situation was better than that of many because I was never homeless, but it was still pretty bad. Commercial Drive became my safety net, providing me with friends and neighbours and lots of free entertainment. Some of the business owners came to know me and helped me in little ways that endeared them to me and made me very loyal in later days.

In those days the building I was living in did not have a lock on the front door, which I found very charming given that I had come back from New York City where people double and triple bolted their doors! Those of us living in the building looked out for each other, our pets and our plants. Life was pretty good and I was starting to get back on track and looking for work, but money was extremely tight.

Then one day, without fanfare or warning, envelopes containing small amounts of cash started to appear under my apartment door. Try to imagine what a feeling that gave me! It was such an unexpected and incredible gesture that it gave me a lift right out of my depression. I suspected that these magic envelopes were coming from building residents but when I quizzed them, to try to thank them, no-one would admit to giving me the envelopes or to seeing anyone putting them under my door. Keep in mind that because there was no lock on the front door the envelopes could have come from anyone, and to this day I still have no idea who was so kind as to give me these invaluable gifts.

Once I was back on my financial feet, the envelopes stopped coming, so it has to have been a person or persons who knew my situation and reached out to lend an anonymous hand. If someone reading this all these years later was the responsible party please know that your gestures were very much appreciated, gave me hope and will never be forgotten.

This experience helped to bond me to the neighbourhood and I am still here!

MONICA DARE

Raising Families on McSpadden

It was a snowy day on April 26, 1975 when we arrived in Vancouver from our little barrio in the Philippines. It was the first time any one of us had ever seen snow. I was not even 2 years old. My mother, Julita, my brothers Federico, Mario, Julius, Ferdinand and my sister Eva travelled over 6,000 miles to be reunited with our two older sisters, Clarita and Merlyn, who had already immigrated here to study nursing. Our Auntie Sylvia and Uncle Dave, along with their two kids, welcomed our whole family into their home on McSpadden Avenue. Twelve people sharing one house. That was a common household where we came from.

This is actually my mother's story. The few years leading up to this move, my mother had gone through the passing of her father, her oldest son and her husband. In addition to that, she only discovered she was pregnant with me three months after my father had passed. She was a 45 year old pregnant widow. The year after I was born, she and my aunt had discussions about moving the family to Vancouver. My Auntie Sylvia, along with my Uncle Dave, was the first in our family to immigrate here. She was the first Filipino registered nurse in BC and my Uncle Dave was an established electrician. They sponsored all of us. They gave us a home, clothed us, fed us and taught us how to live this new way of life.

Although my mother was educated, her years at Union College in Manila could not assist her for a life in Canada. At 47 years old, she attended Vancouver Community College to study English and took a Homemaking course which allowed her to work as a Care Aide in nursing homes. She worked two or three jobs a day, seven days a week doing part-time cleaning gigs at Hotel Vancouver, The Hyatt Regency and also private homes on the west side. Soon, she earned enough money to buy a home... right across the street from my Aunt's house on McSpadden Avenue. It was a perfect neighbourhood close to schools, parks, grocery shopping and public transportation.

We all attended the schools in the neighbourhood – Queen Victoria Elementary, Grandview Elementary, Britannia Secondary, Gladstone Secondary and Van Tech. We enjoyed the area a lot, however it was given a bad reputation especially for being on the east side. It was a convenient location, affordable and very family oriented. There was a sense of community. Although we experienced some culture shock, during the 70s and 80s there were a lot of new immigrants living in the neighbourhood, especially on our block – Chinese, Vietnamese, Portuguese, Italian, etc. We weren't the only ones going through this. I remember going to shop at Patel's (now Dollar Grocers) a lot with my mom. It was run by a Fijian family and she loved the fact that they carried many items that she was familiar with cooking back home, especially their vegetables. I loved it because they gave me lollipops!

After arriving 20 years before, mom made the final mortgage payment on the house in 1995. She was 66 years old and a homeowner. She was no longer working and most of my siblings were settled into their own places with their families. Actually, she was a part-time babysitter and part-time gallivanter. If she wasn't gardening or walking The Drive, she was either square dancing or hanging out with her crew at the Philippine Diamond Society which was a social club for Filipino seniors.

In addition to becoming a homeowner, she was grandmother to 23 grandchildren and most were under her care for many years. Family called her 'mommy baket' which basically meant grandma in Filipino.

In her 30 years of being a resident here, she witnessed the building of the Skytrain, Il Mercato Mall, the moving in of Starbucks, Wonderbucks and McDonald's. Although the face of the area is ever changing, the one thing that remains constant is the community feel of The Drive. I remember knowing all the kids on my block and coming and going to neighbours' houses. My husband and I love this area and we both pride ourselves on being raised here. It's now a 'destination' because of the small shops, restaurants and fun events that are hosted here, including the original Car Free Day and the Parade of Lost Souls street festival. A long time ago families didn't really have a choice about settling into this neighbourhood but now they do. Now it's my turn to raise our family here and the house on McSpadden is perfect to do just that. Thanks Mom.

DIVINA SORIANO LEACOCK

Roll Out the Barrel

In the late 1970s my husband Paul and I were renting a small house near UBC. The landlord was happy to rent to two adults and a well-behaved dog, but he was not so pleased when we had two babies in 17 months and my teenaged sister and her dog moved in with us after my parents died. At this moment of extreme stress, he notified us that we had to leave and we were suddenly thrown into the rental market where, no surprise, no landlord was willing to rent to a family of five with two dogs.

When we went into a real estate office to see what we could buy in Vancouver for under $60,000, we were greeted with incredulity and the sage advice that nothing in that price range was likely to turn up in our lifetime. As born and bred New Yorkers who didn't even own a car at that time, we were resistant to the idea of living in the suburbs. Four days after our discouraging visit to the real estate office, magic happened. The realtor phoned to say that a 'fixer upper' had come up for $59,900 in East Vancouver. When we found out that it was located in our very favourite neighbourhood, Commercial Drive, our faith in karma was restored. We had found a home on Rose Street, where we were meant to be, and our family's lives have been enriched for the past 31 years by this serendipity.

In 1980, the first wave of Italians who had come to the area after the War were moving 'onward and upward', many to larger homes in north Burnaby. We bought our house from one of these families and forged wonderful friendships with the Italians who remained in the neighbourhood.

We have learned much from all our neighbours over the years, and one of the local traditions we embraced most enthusiastically was backyard winemaking. Luigi and Onorina Steffanuci, who had been our friend Mike's next door neighbours all his life, had brought the winemaking tradition with them when they arrived in Vancouver from Italy. A group of local families, led by Mike and often overseen by Luigi, began making wine in his garage and, decades later, our children have joined in this tradition.

For us, the arrival of the grapes from the Okanagan is as much a sign of autumn as the turning of the leaves. Just like the first crocuses of spring, the first oak barrels rolled out into the lane and washed out with a garden hose herald a new season.

When the pickup truck of grapes reaches the lane, our crew is ready. We set up the crusher, an electric version of the old mangle washing machine, pry open the crates and drop the bunches of grapes one by one into the crusher while the dogs snap at the inevitable wasps. We watch as the gorgeous purple globes become pulp and juice, filling huge plastic buckets that will sit in Mike's garage fermenting for a week before the wine is pressed and stored in oak barrels for a year. Neighbours who have absolutely no interest in wine stop by to watch and chat.

When all the grapes have been crushed, the seeds, sludge and stems taken away by delighted composters, and the lane washed down, the potluck lunch begins. On a table in the garage, cheeses, meats, breads, homemade pickles, fruit, biscotti and other delights appear. Accompanied by samples of past vintages and thoroughly enjoyed by the sticky, tired, but always hopeful winemakers, this working lunch is the highlight of the fall season in our little corner of Grandview Woodland and one of the many reasons we are grateful to be living here.

EILEEN MOSCA

Joe's Café

My wife and I and our three small dogs live just off Commercial Drive, a few doors from Joe's Café.

Joe's Café is easily recognized by its classic mural – a rainbow ending in a pot-of-gold cappuccino. As featured in the mural, Joe's is famous for coffees with heads on them that are almost two inches above the top of the cup, Joe's own innovation.

Joe's Café, 1150 Commercial Drive, Vancouver

Joe's Café is on the east side of Commercial Drive at William Street. It is on the northeast corner of the intersection, which is kitty-corner from Grandview Park.

It wasn't until the 1970s that Commercial Drive became the original strip of coffee culture in Vancouver. Most non-Italian Vancouverites found the original Italian coffee shops a bit too ethnic and daunting, and certainly in the 1980s most Vancouverites had never had a cappuccino. The early Italian coffee bars catered to Italian immigrants from the different cities and provinces of Italy: Abruzzo, Roma, Napoli and Calabria. These places live on as the Abruzzo Cappuccino Bar, Café Roma, Caffé Napoli, and the Café Calabria. They are located on Commercial Drive in the same order they are in Italy – Abruzzo and Roma in the north, and then heading south, Napoli and finally, Calabria in the foot of the boot of Italy.

Nevertheless, since 1976 Joe's Café has been the original site of non-Italian coffee culture on 'The Drive.' Joe Antunes is Portuguese, and his place is the largest, with the most diverse clientele. Joe is still there and has 47 stitches from the butt of a bull to attest to the fact he used to be a bullfighter in Portugal.

By the 1980s Joe's was a major hangout for local artists, musicians, gays, film industry people, left-wingers and ordinary folk. Sarah McLaughlin busked in front of Joe's and spent a lot of time playing pool there before becoming famous. Colin James lived in the old apartment building directly behind Joe's and spent a lot of time at Joe's even after he became famous. In 2011 he was still mentioning Joe's Café in banter at his concerts.

In 1983 Joe's brother Tony was surprised to see pictures of two regular customers splashed all over the newspapers. They had just been arrested as part of the Squamish Five – Canada's first group of 'urban terrorists.' Another radical Drive resident at this time was John Jacobs, one of the key founders of the Weather Underground. In Greenwich Village Jacobs had just left the group in a townhouse while they were assembling a bomb when there was a massive explosion that killed three of the group. Jacobs fled the US and eventually ended up hiding in plain sight just off Commercial Drive.

Joe's Café, the play

In 1988, the year I moved to William Street a few doors up from Joe's, musician Wyckham Porteous wrote a play called Joe's Café. It was nominated for a Jessie for Outstanding Original Play. The infamous first producer of the Rolling Stones, Andrew Loog Oldham, produced Porteous' latest album. This new work, 3AM, led to three nominations at the 2008 Canadian Folk Music Awards. Porteous still lives just up William Street.

In September 1990 Joe's Café made the major newspapers over an incident involving two lesbians being thrown out of the café. According to various news articles Joe asked two women to stop their prolonged kissing, and finally got them to leave.

Commercial Drive had become a major lesbian community in Vancouver without many of the public knowing about it. This incident became a rallying point for lesbian solidarity, and a boycott of Joe's Café was announced. This then led to the formation of a volunteer-run lesbian alternative coffee shop named Josephine's, one block away from Joe's on Charles Street, just off Commercial Drive. Echoing the groundbreaking Stonewall incident in New York City's Greenwich Village, this smaller event still served to rally the lesbian community to publicize their presence and their rights, and to demonstrate strength against anti-gay sentiments. Many non-gay people in the neighbourhood supported the protests and actions to some degree.

For years after, the annual Dyke March down Commercial Drive would make a point of protesting in front of Joe's.

I lived by Joe's during the incident, and I feel I should add a fact to the story, in Joe's defense. Despite being a rather quiet and conservative immigrant, Joe actually supported the presence of gay and lesbians in his café, who were a significant part of his business. This is demonstrated by the fact that just before the boycott he had written a $1,000 cheque to buy uniforms and equipment for Vancouver's lesbian baseball team, the Commercial Drive Drivers. This was to assist them in their entry into the international Gay Games (the 'Gay Olympics') that were held a few weeks before in Vancouver. The uniforms had a large 'Joe's Café' logo on them. In response to the boycott he put a copy of the $1,000 cheque in his café's window by the front door for all to see.

In 2011 I interviewed Joe about the kissing incident. He maintained there was no kissing involved in the incident, although lesbians frequently kissed in his café. At the time he employed a young female waitress, but some lesbian customers were grabbing the girl's legs and saying they wanted to go out with her. The waitress had a boyfriend and complained to the man on the coffee machine, saying she wouldn't deliver coffee any more. In response he threw the offending women out. This resulted in a heavy boycott of Joe's, sometimes with protestors blocking the entrance.

In 1997 an article in Xtra West announced the boycott appeared to be over and "Lesbians are returning in increasing numbers to Joe's Continental Coffee Bar."

In the 1990s KD Lang, Colin James and 54-40 would go to Joe's to get their regular coffee hit or play pool. This was the time when a mural was painted along the entire length of Joe's sunny, south-facing wall on William Street. The wall was an instant hit, with dozens of coffee addicts regularly lounging in the sun along its length. It became a favourite spot for photo and video shoots. In 1992 the Ludwigs included the song *Indecent at Joe's Café* on their *Idle and Undesirable* album. This was before the Internet, and before everyone became addicted to expensive coffee.

A version of part of the large 1990s mural on Joe's Café's south wall on William Street

Actress Jennifer Beals lived a few doors up William Street from Joe's in 2006. She had become famous with the 1983 movie *Flashdance*, and was in Vancouver to star in the TV series *The L Word*. Beals wrote an article for *EnRoute Magazine*, titled "Actress Jennifer Beals' Commercial Drive" in which she included a description of Joe's Café:

> "Joe's Café: The Drive is so ethnically diverse and driven by music and people and soccer. I used to live in the area, and during the World Cup, it's just so alive. Joe's Café is a popular place for games, and they have great coffee."

.As Beals points out, Joe's is one of the main places to watch sports, especially hockey games and soccer games. As various teams advance through the soccer World Cup playoffs, thousands of ethnic fans take over the street and celebrate for blocks along Commercial Drive.

Looking south from in front of Joe's Café, 2009

... who is trying to get motivated to finish a book on the uniquenessess of Grandview and Commercial Drive.

La Quena Coffee House

La Quena was a project of the Canadian Latin American Cultural Society (CLACS) and thrived on Commercial Drive for 18 years. It was a free space for social, educational and cultural events, and was also used for organizing, holding meetings, and benefits. Solidarity with people struggling against poverty and oppression was a main theme. Initially the focus was on peoples of Chile, and money raised helped organizations that fought against that most brutal dictatorship. La Quena expanded over time to include solidarity with environmentalism, First Nations, women, labour and unions, farm workers, African National Congress, Nicaragua, El Salvador, Guatemala, Honduras, Philippines, Cuba, Burma, Argentina, Mexico and Ireland.

The initial planning committee was composed of Canadians and exiled Chileans who fled the brutal US-backed dictatorship in their homeland. The committee worked to form La Quena, which opened its doors in October 1982 after more than 100 people volunteered their time to renovate the space at 1111 Commercial Drive.

People from all over the lower mainland worked in La Quena. Over the years there were more than a thousand people donating hours of labour to cook, serve, clean, set up, manage the stage, organize events, and coordinate the whole works. Because La Quena was non-racist, non-sexist, and non-homophobic, people who had been on the fringes of society found a place where they could be themselves and participate in a more inclusive community. As well, people overcame their political differences to come together to fight for equality, democracy and an end to poverty and exploitation.

La Quena was honoured to host great music from the resistance movement. Every Friday and Saturday night, we had a performance. We hosted Roy Bailey on many occasions as he sang of the struggles of people overcoming injustice and inequality. Other English performers were Leon Rosselson and Rory Mcleod. We had many groups and performances of Latin American musicians. We were privileged to hear the ancient cultural music of the Andes, flutes, pan pipes, charangos, and drums. Kin Lalat of Guatemala also performed many times along with Ache Brazil, Mexico's Mez Me. We hosted performers who sang original, traditional and contemporary folk music. Canadian groups included those from Quebec, the Vancouver Men's Chorus, Euphonimously Feminists, Lowry Olafson, Wykham Porteous, Veda Hille, The Tools, Routs Round Up and Stephen Fearing. American folk, jazz and blues singers performed, including the great Sy Kahn. First Nations performers were often present and one familiar singer was David Campbell, who blended the struggles of First Nations peoples of Canada with those of all the Americas. Colombia, Katari Taiko, Cabaret, performed along with many visits from Ngoma. The list seems endless.

A regular event was Open Stage, where community people were invited and encouraged to perform either music or poetry. The 3-tier entrance fee was an innovation, where we offered different rates for employed, under-employed and unemployed.

Individuals, groups and representatives from organizations educated us with regular updates and/or educational talks. We were honoured to have representatives from the Chilean resistance, the Sandinistas of Nicaragua, of the FMLN from El Salvador, and speakers from Mexico, Honduras, Cuba, Peru, to name a few. Amazingly Caesar Chavez from the US farm workers presented us with an update. We also hosted speakers from other parts of the world: Ireland, Israel and Palestine, East Timor, Libya, Philippines and South Asia. In February, during Black History Month, we hosted performers and speakers. Many women's groups also spoke. Meetings were held by Vancouver Association for survivors of torture.

Some of the most interesting art work hung from the walls of the coffee house as well as sculpture; one was a delightful sculpture of people working in La Quena holding up a cup of cappuccino!. Political art, mainly with a message of resistance, was changed monthly. One show was from the Soviet Union. We hosted poetry readings, the literary Olympics, and the Vancouver Industrial Writers Union. Spoken Word performed at La Quena. Theatre in the Raw, a grassroots, ear-to-the-ground independent theatre performed 125 acts deemed 'unusual, engaging and awaking theatre'.

We showed films that usually do not make it on the regular film circuit. Many were documentaries. These were both Canadian and international, showing us about the situation of First Nations people in the series History of Resistance (Oka and You are on Indian Land). Other films covered such diverse topics as Eritrea, Cuba, Uruguay, Rigobert Menchu, Malcolm X, and underdevelopment (presented by IDERA). We showed films by the National Film Board and Vancouver Status of Women, as well as holding an Anarchist Film Night, and Canadian Cinema Nights.

Perhaps the most popular and well publicized event La Quena held was the annual Fiesta. This event started in 1987 and continued for 8 years. It was held in Grandview Park. The day featured incredible music, dancing, speeches and a wide assortment of food. Each year featured a theme; for example, the 7th Fiesta was dedicated to 500 Years of Indigenous Resistance and another took the theme of Think Globally, Act Locally. Community and other solidarity groups set up information tables. These tables included information from Rape Relief, Iran, Lamont and Spencer, Leonard Pelletier committee, Women's Bookstore, OXFAM, Amnesty International, Green Peace, Philippine Women's Centre, Spartacus Books, to name a few.

Throughout the years we held other dances and parties at the coffee house. We were treated to Tango performances by Oscar Nieto. Celebrations for the Day of the Dead, May Day, and New Years took place annually.

Although women played a huge and obvious role in La Quena, we also focused on women-specific issues. We heard the music of Euphoniously Feminists along with many women singers. We provided the space for Women and Words, Women's Health Collective, Midwifery task force, South African Women's committee, Guatemalan women's group (to raise money for art projects for children of working women), Iranian women's issues, South Asian Women's Action network, Women's Prisoners' rights and other educational events.

A group of workers put together a place for children to play while their parents gathered for a coffee and talk with other caregivers. We held Easter and Halloween parties. The kids were treated to piñatas, story telling, face-painting, crafts, and shows. During the Fiesta, we held a children's parade.

Vancouverites were treated to Latin American food, often for the first time, at very reasonable prices. They feasted upon empanadas y pebre, rice, beans, tacos, salads, and special soups. We had some of the most heavenly cheesecake ever. And some La Quena volunteers even learned to make cappuccinos as well as those served in other coffee houses on The Drive!

Those who worked in La Quena believed in creating a better living and working environment through community activism. To that end, we provided space for others to use. The list is long and unfortunately not complete. Here is a sampling: benefits for Pacific Tribune, Green Party, Co-op radio, Unlearning Racism, International Women's Day, Industrial Workers of the World, Tools for Peace, Peace Brigade to Cuba, Friends of Cuba, and Burmese refugee camp. Community participants joined with other organizations to call for comprehensive curbside recycling as well as expressed their opposition to high rises in the Drive neighbourhood. Educationals and benefits were held for East End Co-op, bicycle benefit, Latin American Connexions, Co-development Canada, Kinesis, medical marijuana, Committee for equality for immigrants and new Canadians, West Coast Mental Health, Jean Fortin, mid-wife task force, Environmental crossroads, Aquelarre Women's magazine, Kinesis, Environmental Emergency Response Team (assess war pollution), prison justice day, 'Wyse, Wyld Womyn', Little Sisters Poetry Reading, Women's Health Collective, Men speaking with men about sexism, Child care societies, Central American Student Alliance, Western Canadian Wilderness Committee, Irish committees, Vancouver World AIDS group, Lesbian and Gay groups, Better Environmentally Sound Transportation, Downtown Eastside Poets, International PEN gathering (release imprisoned writers).

La Quena was an incredible success in showing us what the collective power of the people could accomplish. Each one of us who worked at La Quena has great stories to tell.

GRANDVIEW WOODLAND IS AWESOME BECAUSE…

...of the people and the culture. I've been here a year and not a lot of people make judgments – everyone seems to get along. Most people have an open mind – easy breezy attitude. You see the same faces so it feels like community. The Drive is not Kits and not a corporation. People are doing things for themselves – all the independent businesses. It's down home.
(Sean)

Disability, this Ability

My father drives to our evening swim at Templeton pool. Driving is a strain on my father who suffers from Parkinson's. I am afraid of driving. Something else I can add to the growing list of things I feel guilty about. My vocabulary is punctuated with the words: I CAN'T as in I can't do this. I can't work. I can't function. I can't remember. I can't forget.

My father slides the car into the disabled parking lot. We wade through the mundane sameness of our days.

I stand under the shower enjoying the hot jet of water drumming my brain. Recovering from a psychotic episode, I feel lobotomized, slowly reclaiming what arable peace of mind I have left. Surrounded by naked older men, my body is younger than theirs but my illness has aged me. My soul is old and tired. My mind gone to seed.

Dullness, I tell myself, is good for me. The mindless meditative laps back and forth across the pool free my mind from the ceaseless treadmill of habitual worrying that has become my life.

I join my father in the sauna. Sweating away in a cloud of steam, I meet Sean, a teacher from Ireland who frequents the pool. Sean has a story for me:

"Two guys in wheelchairs meet in a pub. They have a friendly conversation. One wheels away, stands up and does a dance to the amusement of his friends. His wheelchair act is just a practical joke. The wheelchair bound guy watches unamused and summons him over. The guy saunters over. The guy in the wheelchair grabs him by the collar and Beats-The-Living-Shit-Out-Of-Him!" Sean leans in. "Never pretend to be disabled to someone who is truly disabled."

He has called my bluff. I am exposed as a fraud. Cowering in the shadows, I seek refuge in my sickness, blaming society for my fears. I've had enough of my hard luck stories. Sick to death of my self-pity. Feeling sorrow for myself going on and on and on about my mental health. My father doesn't allow his Parkinson's to stop him from living. I need to find the everyday courage to 'keep on keeping on' To know the world you have to embrace it. Especially on days you can't bear to face it.

These days I take on too much to prove to myself what I can do with this ability. There is nothing I can't do within my limitations and most limitations are imaginary. I go back to school, I volunteer, facilitate wellness workshops, I do peer support work. I eventually get a job as a mental health worker at a mental health drop-in center where I used to be a client. I start making documentary films again. I do everything I can, trying to make up for my previous low self-esteem. And I burn myself out. I realize now the key is balance. I don't have to prove myself to anybody, not even myself. I need to remind myself that I contribute in the way I know how as best as I can for I am born outside normalcy. Beyond the confines of conformity, beyond honouring the work I do, I honour my abilities and myself. I am not a prisoner of my fears anymore. I am free!

KAGAN GOH

DID YOU KNOW....

DSM IV: Symptoms of Depression:

"A decrease in energy level is invariably present, and is experienced as sustained fatigue even in the absence of physical exertion. The smallest tasks seem difficult or impossible to accomplish. The sense of worthlessness varies from feelings of inadequacy to completely unrealistic negative evaluations of one's worth. The individual may reproach himself or herself for minor failings that are exaggerated and search the environment for cues confirming the negative self-evaluation. The sense of worthlessness or guilt may be of delusional proportions."

Photo courtesy of Kelley Montgomery

Messengers of Hope

A colourful community art project, entitled Messengers of Hope: Living and Playing Hand in Hand, was unveiled at Macdonald Elementary School, in Vancouver's East End, on the last day of classes. The project was the result of more than 1,000 hours of volunteer work over the last year and a half.

It comprises 450 wooden hands traced from each child in the school and preschool, as well as parents, staff, and community members. The hands were cut from plywood and then painted by the children. Mounted on the chain-link fence surrounding the playground, the hands encircle the school, as if to protect and embrace the children within.

Representatives of the Chinese and Vietnamese parents addressed the assembly, and Velma Wallace spoke on behalf of the First Nations parents. She thanked community school coordinator Donna Clark for bringing the project to fruition. In thanking activist Mel Lehan, she said, "Mel taught us a lot about how to stand up for our kids' education."

Wallace noted that the colour scheme—red, yellow, black, and white—symbolizes all racial and cultural groups within the community. "It takes a whole community to raise a child, and we'd like to keep working together."

NANCY KNICKERBOCKER

Photo courtesy of Donna Clark

Editor's Note: This article first appeared in *Teacher Newsmagazine*, Volume 12, Number 2, October 1999. Reprinted with permission.

Albert

Grandview Woodland and Commercial Drive in particular is my favourite part of Vancouver. To park my car and walk, enjoying the diverse beehive of cultural activities. The smell of various foods, the sights of every type of person you can imagine from the outlandish dress of some to the typical business men and women. All doing their own thing and co-existing in this microcosm of our world. Every nationality, gender and age are here uninterrupted and free to be themselves. There is always a demonstration of sorts going on, some loud and boisterous but mostly quiet demonstrations of people collecting money or raising funds in the spirit of improving social justice in our community.

So now I get to the title character in this story. It is a story of great tragedy and strength of human spirit that stretches far beyond our little area called Grandview Woodland but throughout all of Vancouver and the world. A story of poverty, addiction, inequality and as I said before a tribute to human strength, generosity and altruism.

I knew my friend Albert from May 2, 1994 to August 4, 2009 when he passed away of exposure and alcohol related illness on a cold rainy night in a park right in front of the bus station in downtown Vancouver. I would like to think he was trying to get on a bus to escape his tortured existence but deep down in my heart I know that he was just trying to survive another night. Some, those that never really knew him, might say that it was a waste of a life.

He was known on The Drive to sit in front of the Royal Bank at First & Commercial panhandling to get enough for his next bottle of Listerine, wine or a hit from a crack pipe. I met my friend in a recovery home for addiction when we were both struggling; surrendering to power much greater than ourselves - Addiction. I have managed to stay sober since then but Albert continued to struggle, losing the battle a little bit at a time. I shed a tear as I write this because Albert was a dear friend and I think I knew him better than most.

Sometimes I would drive right by him and shake my head, smiling or saddened by the sight of him standing or sitting in front of that bank. The community, police and ambulance attendants recognized this man. The Albert Wallace very few people knew was talented, adventurous, caring and giving. He played guitar and sang songs. In the past, he was on the work crew that built the chateau up on Grouse Mountain. He loved to tell the story about how he had had to be rescued from a rock face by North Vancouver Search and Rescue. He loved the horse races and always dreamed of being a professional handicapper writing 'Best Bets by Albert' in the newspaper.

He had a host of friends in the 12 Step community and gave of his time and energy organizing and working hard with little or no pay at the various recovery homes he attended. At the Vancouver Recovery Club, a 24 hour a day establishment, he gave freely of himself and was recognized for his hard work and, for a short time, was the manager.

Albert never spoke of his family; I know he was adopted when he was young. So he used my address because he stayed with me sometimes when he was trying to get sober. They contacted me when they found his body. We had a small gathering of about 30-50 people at the Watari office where he sometimes saw Craig as a counsellor. Alas Albert, that brave and courageous man who almost always had a smile on his face, is buried in an unmarked grave in White Rock. His spirit lives on through the people he helped. I feel like I haven't written enough to honour his great First Nations spirit but his was a short life and I knew only a little.

BARRY CONROY

Macdonald School

Our struggle was long. It started in October 1995 and ended in May 1997 when the Vancouver School Board (VAB) agreed to provide additional staff to address the needs of the students at Sir William Macdonald Elementary School.

Fall 1995

Teachers at Macdonald, an inner-city school in the north-east of Vancouver, met to discuss the desperate unmet needs of our students. The first step was for every teacher to keep a diary for a designated week. We shared these diaries of incredibly compelling stories of events in our students' lives for the week and the significant effects that these had on their behaviour. Our area's assistant superintendent was deeply moved. Teachers agreed to be diligent in demanding the services that our collective agreement required.

During the 1995–96 school year, our school underwent accreditation. We defined as a goal a minimum of two trained adults in every classroom. The external team unanimously supported this. The year before we had completed a "Dynamic Assessment" on all our students. The assessment showed that our students could learn, could be excited by learning, but usually did not have the skills or strategies necessary to make progress. We decided to use this information in a major brief to the school board. Our two learning-assistance teachers reviewed the achievement levels of all our students in a number of areas.

November 1996

We presented the brief to the board. We asked for a pilot project at Macdonald that would provide an additional trained person in every enrolling class. Parents assisted in the presentation. The board thanked us.

As a result of the inaction by the VSB and the escalating problems at Macdonald, the executive of the Vancouver Elementary School Teachers' Association (VESTA) declared Macdonald a "school in crisis." We withdrew our association representatives to many district committees.

The superintendent requested an immediate meeting with our three full-time table officers. We again presented our concerns. The entire staff was present and introduced themselves to the array of assembled trustees and senior management. The board responded by providing, until June, one additional support staff person for the entire school. Not good enough!

February 1997

VESTA, with the financial assistance of the BC Teachers Federation, hired a community organizer. Mel Lehan worked with parents to assist them with strategies and tactics that might successfully result in more support for their children. Parents, staff, and VESTA representatives again met with the board and officials from various ministries, but there was no response from the VSB.

April 2, 1997

In frustration, a group of parents set up a camp on the lawn of the school-board offices and resolved to stay until the needs of their children had been met. They were there for 40 days!

Lana Wright, a parent, decided to walk from Prince Rupert to Vancouver to raise awareness, not just of the unmet needs of the students at Macdonald, but for all other inner-city schools and First Nations children. She began her walk on April 12 and arrived back at Macdonald on June 14.

During this period, most of the teachers and many parents were interviewed on radio, appeared on TV, or were quoted in newspapers. The parents' camp was covered in every local paper, on all Vancouver TV stations, in various union and other newsletters, and even in *The Globe and Mail*.

Mid-May 1997

As a result of these concerted and coordinated actions, the VSB agreed to continue the January to June alternate program worker, and to provide two additional teachers and two additional support staff workers for at least the 1997–98 school year. Through the coordination efforts of the VSB, various ministries and community groups are committed to continue addressing the problems by such actions as developing and locating programs at Macdonald School or in the Macdonald neighbourhood.

It may not be perfect, but all involved believe it's a considerable victory for our students. We hope our efforts can be used to help other teachers and parents address their "in crisis" schools, too.

Editor's Note: Barb Parrott was VESTA 1st Vice-President, a member-at-large on the BCTF Executive, and a teacher at Macdonald Elementary School, Vancouver when she wrote this article for *Teacher Magazine*, Volume 10, Number 1, September 1997. Reprinted with permission.

Kiwassa Neighbourhood House

Kiwassa Neighbourhood House is a grassroots, multi-service community agency that has been providing a broad range of free or low cost social services and programs to children, youth, adults, seniors and families in East Vancouver for 60 years. Kiwassa works in partnership with residents, community agencies, businesses, government and non-government organizations, using a community development and capacity building approach to identify and respond to community needs.

At Kiwassa, we believe that our community members should expect and receive community-based programs and services as defined by community members. Our mission is to provide opportunities that engage, educate and empower people in order for them to participate productively in their community. Kiwassa fosters personal, social and community development.

We strive to identify areas and issues of greatest need within our targeted community, and to initiate programs and services to meet these needs. We strive to bring neighbours together, encouraging them to share their experiences and friendship with each other. We work cooperatively with other agencies to identify, develop and support programs and services offered elsewhere in our community and city.

We are children, youth, adults, and seniors of all ethnicities, beliefs, cultures, abilities, and economic levels. We speak many languages and we are people of all sexual orientations. We value diversity and endeavour to reflect the diversity of our neighbours in our membership, our Board of Directors, our volunteers and our staff. We respect all of our neighbours and we expect that all who come to our House and all of those who provide and receive our services will extend the same respect to all they meet here. In accordance with this, we will act to promote the inclusion of all in our Neighbourhood House and in our community.

Kiwassa was formed in 1949 by the Kiwassa Ladies Club of Vancouver, a service club comprised of the wives and daughters of members of the Kiwanis Club. The Kiwassa Club was concerned about the needs of inner city children, especially girls and their families, and so they fundraised and initiated volunteer led activities for the girls and their parents. The Kiwassa Girls Club, as it was known, was based out of an old fire hall at 600 Vernon Drive, in the Grandview Woodland neighbourhood of East Vancouver.

Kiwassa was developed over time to build on the settlement / neighbourhood house model of providing needed services and community development within a community.

Kiwassa incorporated as a non-profit society in 1951 and was registered as a charitable organization in 1967. Programs continued for girls and expanded to involve all residents. In 1961, the name was legally changed to Kiwassa Neighbourhood Services Association – Kiwassa Neighbourhood House for short.

In 1987, Kiwassa decided it could better meet the needs of the community by relocating from Vernon Drive to the current location at Oxford Street and Nanaimo. Extensive community planning and fundraising was undertaken. The new Kiwassa Neighbourhood House opened its doors in 1992 at 2425 Oxford Street.

The current Kiwassa Neighbourhood House is a purpose-built, 15,500 square foot community facility developed by Kiwassa, with support from all levels of government and a long list of donors. Kiwassa Neighbourhood House's building was given to the City of Vancouver and is leased for $1 per year. Kiwassa Neighbourhood House belongs to the community. The site includes a low-income family housing complex. Kiwassa also operates three licensed childcare programs and one early child development program off site, and also developed and operates a second housing complex in the neighbourhood.

When the Vancouver Kiwassa Club formed and started the Kiwassa Girls Club, the founders took the name Kiwassa because they understood it means "little sister" in an unspecified Aboriginal language. We have also learned that in Cree, Kiwassa has a meaning something like 'extended family'. We think it fits.

Kiwassa Neighbourhood House is governed by a Board of Directors who are community leaders from our neighbourhood volunteering their time to support the work of Kiwassa. Kiwassa board members bring a broad range of skills, experiences and connections to their governance role.

Kiwassa Neighbourhood House has a staff of sixty that reflect the broad diversity within our neighbourhood. Our staff bring an eclectic range of education, professional training and experience to the work of Kiwassa, as well as passion, ideas and energy. Collectively, Kiwassa staff speak 16 languages: English, Cantonese, Mandarin, Spanish, Hindi, Punjabi, Vietnamese, Tagalog, French, Dutch, Polish, Turkish, Taiwanese, Japanese, Cree and sign language.

Kiwassa works closely with a broad range of partners, including our local schools, Hastings Sunrise Community Policing Centre, Hastings Community Centre, Hastings North Business Improvement Association; the Ministry of Children and Family Development, St. David's Church, the Longhouse Ministry, Vancouver Public Library and many other organizations working in our community.

DID YOU KNOW...

There are twenty two coffee shops on Commercial Drive.

Just One Block in Grandview

This is about the one city block where my wife Gail and I live, the 1700 block of William Street.

You may know this block where it meets Commercial Drive at its western edge. The intersection has Joe's Café on its northeast corner, which is kitty-corner from Grandview Park. The buildings in the 1700 block of William are mostly 1910 era homes constructed during the original establishment of Grandview on land that not long before was ancient BC rainforest and First Nations territory.

Commercial Drive is the original strip of coffee culture in Vancouver. Our starting point is Joe's Café, since 1976 the original site of non-Italian coffee culture on 'The Drive.'

I got to know Joe's when I moved to William Street in 1988 when it was a major bohemian hangout for local artists, gays, musicians, film industry people, left-wingers and ordinary folk. In her early days Sarah McLaughlin busked in front of Joe's. KD Lang, Colin James and 54-40 would go to Joe's to get their regular coffee hit in the 1990s. More recently actress Jennifer Beals would frequent Joe's.

The 1700 block William Street

The next building is the 1912 Melton Apartments at 1727 William. The original wood siding is stuccoed over, a testament to the height of the Italian era on The Drive in the 1970s. The top floor apartment on the right side was home to an unknown Colin James around the time he broke through and began opening for Stevie Ray Vaughan. At the same time, the left-hand apartment was home to long-term resident Patrick Pon. As a stunt man and bad guy in the movies, he had a recurring role as 'the Shredder' in the Ninja Turtle TV series.

Skipping a few houses, 1749 William is noteworthy for retaining its original 1909 exterior and being used in a number of TV commercials. It was built for William Jordan, the captain of Fire Hall #5 and holder of badge #4 in the Vancouver Fire Department. It is also where I spent 10,000 hours writing a comprehensive map-based history of Vancouver, *Vancouver: A Visual History*. Other residents in the house include a homeschooling-beekeeping landscaper extraordinaire, and one of the original video editors at *Reboot*, the first half-hour, completely computer-animated TV series.

At Salsbury Drive, we come to the site of one of world-famous Vancouver photographer Jeff Wall's most iconic photos, *The Pine on the Corner* (1990). The image shows the Vancouver Special at 1797 William with a giant unsymmetrical pine tree in its front yard, but sadly the giant pine was cut down in 2007.

Pine on the corner

A longtime neighbour recalls how this lot was the site of the best old house on the block, renowned for its oak interior woodwork. As a small bulldozer knocked the house down, he was almost in tears, at least until the dozer accidentally fell into the basement.

Moving south across William we come to the 1911 Menchions' house, the home of W.R. Menchions from 1911 until he died in 1946. The Menchions Shipyard was located next to where the Bayshore Inn is today on Coal Harbour, and it was one of the best-known wooden shipyards in Canada from 1909-1990.

Heading west down William, we come to the 1910 house at 1768 William, oddly enough the 1950s home of Success Business College. Ten years ago it was splashed on the front page of the Vancouver *Province* when the owner decided to breed wolves behind a chain link fence that ran right out to the sidewalk. A few years ago a scene in a *Twilight Zone* episode was filmed out front starring the Newman character from *Seinfeld*, Wayne Knight. Actress Alisen Down lived there in 2000, when she was playing the autopsy doctor on *Davinci's Inquest* and starring in her own TV series, *Mysterious Ways*. Now it is home to Nisga'a-Haida carver Luke Parnell, two comedians and a naturopathic doctor.

The newest house on the block is 1758 William. The original house here was a cottage built in 1902, the same year the first roads were being constructed in Grandview. The place looked like a vacant lot – mostly lawn with a large tree at the back. Behind the tree the house was positioned right on the back lane. From 1950 it was the home of the Mazurs. Since the house was so full of memories of her family life, Grace Mazur stipulated that her home be torn down after her death. In 2003 a new duplex with a double garage was built in its place. Today the garage seems like the ghost of Grace's 1902 house

1750, 1742 & 1736 William

– it's the same size and shape. The new house became memorable when it was rented out to Jennifer Beals, the famous dancer in the 1983 hit movie *Flashdance*. She was in Vancouver to star in *The L Word* TV series. In 2008 the house was rented out to the assistant director of the second Twilight series movie, *The Twilight Saga: New Moon*.

The next house was home to singer Kinnie Starr, who left in 2003 to do a two-year singing stint with Cirque de Soleil in Las Vegas. Starr is a part Mohawk, trilingual, bisexual, solo artist specializing in Canadian hip-hop and alternative rock. She was nominated for the Juno Award for New Artist of the Year in 2004 and won a Juno for Aboriginal Recording of the Year in 2010 for an album she produced.

For a time the front garden of 1736 William was a big hit with gardening magazines. Only part of that amazing native plant garden is left. Formerly it was full of original Vancouver plants such as huckleberry bushes, skunk cabbages, and an arbutus tree. It featured a rock waterfall and a trout pond filled with a dozen large trout. Its dedicated creator Shawn was a gay man born in Yemen of Iranian ancestry. It was probably Vancouver's best front yard garden of native Vancouver plants.

Old stump, natural garden and 1909 house

Next is 1730 William, a heritage house with its original 1909 dark-stained wood that has been featured in a number of TV commercials. A large 1904 cedar stump dominates its 'natural' front garden. The current owner successfully spent two years working to save the even bigger Hollow Tree in Stanley Park from chain saws.

Shortening up, some other homeowners here include Jack and Irene Fitzgerald who have lived over 60 years in the same house (since 1951), reclusive rock drummer Fisher Rose, a writer working full time on a new theory of physics (wikimechanics.org), a nurse, a school teacher, three civil engineers in a row, and an award winning special effects expert / screenwriter with a total of 8 Emmy, 6 Gemini and 5 Leo nominations.

Back at Commercial Drive, this corner nicely celebrates the progressive ideals of many people in the neighbourhood. In 2005 two residents of the 1700 block William, Sean Osborne and Bruce Macdonald, enlisted the support of 95% of the businesses on Commercial Drive to make Commercial Drive the first Fair Trade Zone in North America, and it was announced at this corner.

Grandview's current Member of Parliament, Libby Davies, lived for years on William Street with her husband, fellow city councillor Bruce Erickson. Libby's father worked to establish Fair Trade in Canada in 1946. Coincidentally the store window of Ten Thousand Villages that faces William Street proclaims the business has been "Fair Trade Since 1946."

BRUCE MACDONALD & GAIL MCDERMOTT,
with almost no help from our three dogs, Leo, Rosie & Pansy

Wall Street Community Garden

Once upon a time (in 1997), there was a little playschool at Chimo Terrace on Wall Street. A parent, a grandparent, and a volunteer at that playschool were asked to meet with Nancy McRitchie, from Kiwassa Neighbourhood House, to talk about community development. So, Chris, Maple, and Jan helped Nancy to interview and hire a Community Development Worker. Lili, age 2, also attended all the meetings and interviews and when we hired Shereen, a lovely young woman originally from Cairo, she said that having a kid at the interview made her feel more relaxed.

We called it the 'Wall Street Healthy Community Project', and the first thing we did was to host a free community picnic in Pandora Park. On huge sheets of paper we asked local residents to write down what they valued about our area, and what they would like to see happen. With Shereen's guidance we had more community meetings and developed the ideas. One thing that we wanted to see was a community garden, so one day Shereen said to me, "Just do it! Write a poster". So I did, by hand, since at the time I didn't have even a passing acquaintance with a computer. We met with residents, we met with the Park Board, and that's how Wall Street Community Garden came to be. With a lot of work from a lot of people to actually build the garden!

That's my best memory from my time in the community, except, of course, for watching my Lili grow up to almost sixteen. But that would be a much longer, and even happier, story.

JAN ROBINSON

Our Grandview Woodland House

One of the reasons we bought our house at 1760 Napier (in 1997) was because of its history. Everyone — the real estate agent, the person selling the house (Joe Maroon), the tenants in the house, the house's former tenants, the neighbours all up and down the block and in a few adjoining blocks — everyone knew this had been 'the doctor's house.' The story was that a doctor, a general practitioner, had lived in the house for decades and had run his practice out of the house. The house's design is quite quirky. On the front porch, you either go straight in the front door, or you enter to your right, through French doors into the 'waiting room.' Beyond the waiting room is the 'examining room'

The story goes that the house was built in 1906 on the third lot from the southwest corner of Salsbury. The doctor owned the first two lots too and, for many years, the first two lots were his rose garden. The doctor had two sons, and when they were old enough to need houses of their own, the good doctor built one small house for each of them, 1117 and 1121 Salsbury Drive. He built them cheek-by-jowl, straddling the lots and set way at the back so they wouldn't ruin his wonderful rose garden. His sons couldn't look into his windows and he wouldn't have to look into theirs.

It turns out there are elements of truth in the story, but some very important elements were not true! In 1998 I attended a neighbourhood workshop on how to research the history of your heritage house at which I received some handy tips about what to look for in the archives, how to gather clues. I went off to the archives to find out more about 'the doctor'. After several false starts — I couldn't find our address, 1760 Napier, in City Directories for 1906, 1907, 1908, 1909, 1910 — I took the chance of looking up the Salsbury address of one of the supposed son's house and it was there! Then I looked back and back and found that both the 'sons' houses' (1117 and 1121 Salsbury) had been built in 1906 by a real estate developer named Charles Reid (of Lennox Reid & Co. lvs., called a 'broker' in some of the City Directories, with an office at 922 Burrard, in 1910, and at 508 Dunsmuir in 1917), not by a GP.

Charles Reid lived at 1121 Salsbury for a few years after he built it. He was also the 'architect and builder' of our house at 1760 Napier and a building permit was issued for our house 8 Jan 1910. After 1760 Napier was completed, Mr. Reid moved into it (and resided in it from at least 1910 to 1914). He then sold it to a dentist, Dr. Arthur W. Greenius (rhymes with Dennis), in approximately 1914.

Dr. Greenius had his office in the building on the southeast corner of Commercial at First Avenue (#2, 1704 East First), so he was able to walk to work, and his family lived at 1760 Napier from 1914 until about 1957. He had two children, a daughter Myrtle and a son Wilmer. Wilmer later became a dentist as well and much later moved to 1638 Charles St.

Arthur's father was James Greenius, a blacksmith, who had his shop at 480 Keefer St., and Arthur's brother was Reuben O. Greenius, an engineer, who also lived at 480 Keefer (and was listed in 'active service', probably serving in World War I, in 1917) who lived to be 96.

Dr. Greenius's daughter Myrtle was about 4 when, in 1914, her family took up residence at 1760 Napier. Wilmer was born soon thereafter. Myrtle lived in the house until she was married, at the Presbyterian Church at 1795 Napier across the street, in 1939 (The church is a BC Mills prefab, built in the same era as 1760 Napier, and is now the only BC Mills prefab church left in Vancouver).

Dr. Greenius owned the two little houses on Salsbury Drive, and when Myrtle and Wilmer were ready to leave the family home, each of them got one of the Salsbury houses. So their children grew up next door to their grandparents.

In about 2000, I tracked down Myrtle, who was quite elderly, and her daughter Irene, who was a BC Transit bus driver, and had them over for tea to let them see the old house and reminisce. Irene had grown up in 1121 Salsbury.

In about 2004 I located Wilmer's two daughters, Fran and Ev, who lived in different towns in the Interior, and they came to spend a weekend with us. They grew up in 1117 Salsbury and hadn't been in our house, their grandparents' house, since 1957. We had such a good time with them and they brought all their family photos and shared them with us. I scanned a few for posterity.

The green space and the two BC Mills prefab houses, 1117 and 1121 Salsbury, that used to be on the southwest corner of Napier and Salsbury were, for most of the 20th century, part of the 1760 Napier property. Arthur W. Greenius did have his rose garden there; photos show the Greenius' lawn swing in the rose garden.

The two Salsbury houses and the rose garden are gone now. They once straddled what is now two city lots. When they were built, however, it was typical of houses along Salsbury to be oriented to face Salsbury and not to face the east-west streets. About three years ago the two BC Mills houses were demolished and two duplexes were built on the property beside our house, facing Napier.

So, the 'doctor' was a dentist. He had a daughter and a son, not two sons. The Salsbury houses were built a few years before the 'big' house. But there was a rose garden!

Here are Fran and Ev in the 1950s. And when they visited us in about 2004.

The Garden the Community Loved

The corner of Salsbury and Napier, one block from busy Commercial Drive, was once the site of a beautiful garden known as the Salsbury Garden. It was also the site of a determined two year struggle by the community to try and save it from a developer's bulldozer. That was back in 2006-07 and also where I had the privilege of living between 1989 and 2006.

The Greenius family, who lived next door on Napier until the 1950s, first established the Salsbury Garden in 1914. Over the years, the garden grew into a true heritage garden, unique in so many ways. Conifer trees that were planted around the edges had by 2007 grown into towering giants in which crows and raccoons nested. An oversize laurel hedge created a dense enclosure from the surrounding streets and, within the garden, a magnificent butternut tree, which fed the squirrels, grew surrounded by diverse perennial and shade gardens, berry bushes, vegetable gardens, and a fishpond. The garden attracted dozens of bird species and was a truly beautiful place.

The garden was also an important community space for the many nearby residents who frequented the garden. It was not uncommon to see strangers sitting at the picnic table enjoying the tranquility of the setting. I remember an elderly man who I sometimes saw snoozing in a garden chair in the early morning. Even a few homeless folks found shelter among the laurel underbrush where they could sleep unbothered. One particular homeless man who I knew for a short time helped me clean up garden debris as a gesture of appreciation for the garden. Dozens more friends and neighbours helped build a small cob guesthouse in a corner of the garden, which became a garden attraction and refuge for friends seeking temporary accommodation.

Equally unique at the Salsbury Garden site were two small BC Mills prefab homes built in 1907 and regarded as valuable heritage buildings. Along with the garden, they were listed on Heritage Vancouver's 2006 top 10 endangered sites in Vancouver.

My roommates and I always encouraged visitors to the garden who often remarked how peaceful and tranquil it felt. The feeling of being out of the city was why the garden felt so

extraordinary and I came to understand the garden as an important ecological niche and green space within the neighbourhood that afforded people the opportunity to reconnect with nature.

Sadly, few sizable gardens from earlier times remain in Grandview Woodland and, except for a few hidden away that remind us of a more pastoral past, most heritage gardens are now gone.

In 2005, development pressures and housing prices in the area were hitting all-time highs and we began to fear that the valuable Salsbury Garden on its large corner lot would soon be sold since the owner was getting on in age. Sure enough, one day without notice, a developer came knocking with an eviction notice in hand. The struggle to save the garden began.

The important story here is the extent to which the community came together to try and save the garden. It was no surprise that the community cared so much, especially those who had spent time in the garden over the years. We understand the importance of green space and we are a community that is willing to take action against its loss.

My roommate, our next door neighbours and nearby residents formed the Friends of Salsbury Garden. We collected over 1600 signatures on a petition. A large block party was organized to celebrate the garden. The media was contacted and wrote stories about our efforts. We temporarily defeated our eviction from home and successfully lobbied our government representatives at all three political levels to help us save the garden. Momentum was building fast and we grew optimistic that a fair resolution with the developer would be achieved when the City Council at the time decided to purchase the property as a community park. Unfortunately the City's very fair offer along with the community's vocal plea to save the garden failed to pry the property loose from a developer intent on making big profits through redevelopment.

Frustrated and not having the money the developer wanted, we had little choice but to appeal the development permit through the Board of Variance. An exhaustive appeal was prepared. In January 2006 about 70 supporters crammed into the small and dreary Board of Variance meeting room where we anxiously but persuasively presented our case. On one side was our assorted crowd of residents and, across the table, the developer and his lawyer. It was a spectacle, which I am certain impressed upon the Board members just how much we cared about this humble little property.

We prepared a scale model representation of the space before and after along with a video of the garden with passionate interviews. Expert witnesses were brought in and we argued that the loss of this garden and homes represented an irreversible loss of important community heritage and green space. We knew our arguments were important and sincere, but it still felt like a David and Goliath challenge given the legal protection most developments have.

Four hours later and after hearing all sides, including the City Development Office who issued the permit and argued in support of the developer, the four Board members decided by a simple vote. The final vote - three in our favor, one against. A loud gasp erupted. We were all stunned and in this moment it felt like democracy had truly triumphed. Without a doubt it was one of the most thrilling and joyful moments of my life. The community had beaten the developer and we felt jubilant.

With the developer's permit now quashed and no opportunity for the developer to appeal the BoV decision, we were certain that we had won the struggle. Sadly however, our hard fought victory was short lived.

Rather than giving up the property, the developer took the issue to the BC Supreme Court resulting in a further two year legal challenge. This higher court ultimately ruled that the powers of the Board of Variance do not allow for 'third party;' appeals. This effectively overruled the BoV decision. The developer was reissued his permit and proceeded with the development. The decision revoked a very important right that Vancouver residents historically had to challenge unwanted developments in their neighbourhoods. The decision was a big win for developers and big loss for Vancouver citizens. But this is another story.

Still not about to give in, the community stepped up its actions and attempts to buy out the developer, but by now the developer was totally unwilling to give in to us rowdy, tree loving residents. So it was that sometime in 2007, early one morning while most people were still asleep, the bulldozers moved in. A few of us managed to get to the site quickly (I had long since been evicted) and blocked the machines, but once the police arrived there was nothing we could do but painfully watch the homes and trees get razed to the ground.

A few smaller trees still remain and in place of the garden now sit two duplexes with large double garages. It is hard to imagine that a magnificent garden once grew at the corner of Salsbury and Napier, but for those of us who spent time in the garden, our fond memories of the Salsbury Garden will always remain.

Home

I have now lived in British Columbia for ten years. Thinking back to when I first came here, it seems only yesterday when I first began my journey. Through the experience of moving to British Columbia and living here, I am more self-aware and continue on this enlightening path while appreciating the beauty and diversity of this place I now call home.

I come from a small place in Nova Scotia. Well, if you want to be specific, "Great Village". I know, I know, where is this place you're asking. Well, look at a map and check out the Bay of Fundy. I love Nova Scotia and have a beautiful family that lives there but I wanted to see what else was in Canada and, in particular, Vancouver. I was 22 years old on my final trip with friends across Canada (destination Vancouver), this time determined to make it out west. A couple of my other attempts were not so successful but definitely life-changing and much appreciated life experiences.

The story continues – my friends and I make it to Vancouver and are staying in a house on Woodland and Commercial Drive with friends. My first thought was this place is amazing, all of the different people, languages and food; it seemed like there was a vibrant static to the air which took you into its embrace in one big squeeze. So much DIVERSITY I wanted to scream; this is what I was looking for, in this place I could be me and have a bit of anonymity. The people were easy to talk to, the shops were never ending with all the hippy-loving feel and trinkets from around the world. Not to mention the coffee - the first time I took a sip of real coffee was on Commercial Drive. Nothing beats an espresso; it transforms you to a land of coffee lovers.

With the help of friends and community around Commercial Drive, I found employment, integrated myself into this new world and have been here ever since. I no longer live around Commercial Drive but still love going there for a cup of coffee, to visit the intriguing shops and to listen to some music that will keep you spinning. I feel that this unique community allowed me to feel comfortable, brave and welcome into a world that was unknown to me. At first feeling anxious and afraid of being in a new place, I instead came to appreciate and love this small-town feel in a big city, with such a sense of community, diverse culture, mountains, unique people and coffee. I was home.

MARCIA GAMBLE

Commercial Health Centre

Just before 2002 I moved into a cockroach-infested house on 11th Avenue, between Commercial and Woodland in Vancouver. I'd been living in Penticton for a year and a half because I couldn't find any heroin there and that was supposed to make life easier, but frankly the removal of drugs didn't make a whole lot of difference. Things weren't going too well with my girlfriend either, and then one morning on CNN it looked like World War III was going to break out so I said "fuck everything," abandoned my mattress in an alley and caught a Greyhound Bus back to Vancouver.

When I arrived at Main Street terminal I made two phone calls. The first was to my dealer and the second was to my friend Riley for a place to stay. Both of them hooked me up and I spent the next several weeks alternately high or withdrawing on Riley's living room floor. Riley was a sport and didn't give me any flack about all the sweat and vomit, but he was busy at UBC becoming a lawyer and his life choices reflected something in me that I didn't like to face. I needed to secure my own room so I got a job at The Body Shop and as soon as I received my first paycheck I paid the deposit and moved into the house on 11th and Commercial.

My roommates were a couple and my friend who also used heroin. My friend and I helped each other keep our drug use secret from our roommates and teamed up for midnight attacks on the cockroaches. We'd wrap ourselves in garbage bags and take apart the stove armed with aerosol cans.

The house was also infested with mice and almost every night I'd wake up to a mouse screaming, stuck to the sticky pad traps we'd laid out. I'd pick up the sticky pad in one hand and a bottle of olive oil in the other and walk out into the street and pour oil onto the mouse's fur to loosen it from the sticky pad. Later I learned that you have to relocate mice to entirely different neighbourhoods, otherwise they just return to the same house and reclaim their territories. I must have released the same mice dozens of times over because there couldn't have been room inside the walls of that old house for all the mice I released. They just kept coming back and I kept greasing them up and dropping them outside the door, neither of us learning a thing.

There was a sign in a window at Commercial and 11th that said methadone. I was having trouble showing up for work because I was sick from never having enough heroin, so I walked into Commercial Health Centre and asked for a prescription. They asked if there was a history of substance abuse in my family and I said "No, but there's a lot of religion which is very similar," and nobody laughed. Two days later blood work came back to prove my opiate levels and the psychiatrist gave me a prescription for methadone.

Years later, in detox, a guy told me methadone had been invented by Nazi scientists to compensate for wartime opiate shortages and apparently doctors at Stalingrad dispensed daily dosages to soldiers on the front lines to stop them deserting. I don't know if this version of methadone's inception is accurate, but it wasn't difficult to imagine. From the day I started taking methadone, if I stayed away from Commercial Health Centre and the pharmacy at Broadway Station too long, I'd be filled with a need so excruciating and prolonged that heroin withdrawal seemed like a minor head cold in comparison.

From a harm reduction standpoint my life became fairly functional. The house on 11th was sold and we all moved out so the new owners could fix up the place. I moved to Mount Pleasant, worked at a coffee shop on Main Street and enrolled in courses at UBC. I checked in at Commercial Health Centre every week or two and picked up my prescription at Shoppers Drug Mart, first daily, then weekly, and finally, after a succession of clean urine tests, bi-weekly. I probably could've lived that way for years; the only problem was I was dead inside. I'd sit at my computer to do schoolwork and be filled with a paralyzing sense of panic. Summoning words worthy enough to go onto a page felt to me like something only real people did and there was something not quite real about me. Other people's lives affected and involved the world, but mine floated outside.

With the doctor's permission I reduced my methadone dose to a level that was almost a placebo and the receptors in my brain went ballistic. I stopped going to school and holding jobs and started using heroin again. The doctor increased my methadone dose in an attempt to re-stabilize, but there was never much stability in the first place. Inside me was a precipice.

I moved next door to my old, pest-infested house on 11th Avenue. My roommates paid the rent and I sold my books and music for cash and met my dealer on the corner of 11th and Woodland and sat on the front steps and smoked cigarettes.

One rainy evening an SUV ran me down in the intersection at Broadway and Commercial. I'd picked up my methadone at Shoppers Drug Mart and as I headed back home through the crosswalk a vehicle turned east onto Broadway, scooped me up and sent me flying. Witnesses said I sailed 20 feet and landed on my head. Little seizures started blacking out my right eye and I got a lawyer who negotiated an ICBC settlement for $9,000. By the time I received the money I'd moved out of the house on 11th and Commercial and into a studio space on Hastings and Cambie. From there I took the Skytrain to Broadway Station to pick up my methadone and spent more than $100 a day on heroin, trying futilely to numb out the world.

After ten weeks of this routine I ran out of money and for the next eighteen months I thrashed on the hooks of heroin and methadone. I slept on friend's couches, on park benches and in doorways. I checked into shelters, detox and treatment centres. I wandered Vancouver with a backpack and empty dreams.

I was living at The Regal Hotel on Granville Street when I ran into somebody I knew from high school who referred me to her friend who needed to sublet his basement suite at Turner and Victoria. He said he had a good feeling about me and left me with the keys to his house. I appreciated the location because it was close to my methadone resources and I wouldn't have to risk the Skytrain every day without fare.

The last time I used heroin was in that basement suite at Turner and Victoria. I took my last methadone dose a few months later. For a long time after that I didn't like to walk down Commercial Drive because I'd have visceral memories of being wired, but associations change like everything else. This past April my partner and I bought our first property, a townhouse on Lakewood Drive just north of Hastings, and these days rather than roam The Drive derelict I sit on its patios and sip wine, the embodiment of gentrification.

A Yogi on The Drive

In 2007 I arrived in Vancouver on somewhat of a mission. A mission that would in the future cause me many moments of questioning why I had left a life that seemed destined to living, studying and teaching in retreat centre environments for the chaos of urban life. There was a persistent voice that taunted me, it kept saying some variation of, "it's time to take the teachings and practices given to you and step off the yoga mat into the unknown." I had no real idea what this meant. I had been pretty out of touch over the years with what was happening out in 'the real world' but I was aware of the extreme opposites of socio/economic status in Vancouver and the suffering of people who were homeless and dealing with issues related to substance abuse and mental health. So it seemed like Vancouver was the perfect place to begin to look for my answers and figure out what my dharma was to be.

I arrived to be welcomed by friends of a not-so-past life, into their humble abode, a Co-op a few blocks from Commercial Drive. I was happy to be living in this area; I really liked telling people I lived near 'The Drive' as it seemed to reflect the bohemian image I felt comfortable wearing. When I walked down the street I saw an eclectic mix of people from different cultures and ethnic heritages. I felt safe as a queer-identified person and fantasized about a day to come where I would walk down the street with my girlfriend-to-be and hold her hand without consequence.

Some folks I met who had lived in the neighbourhood for many years told me it had become gentrified; high-end stores replace mom and pop shops and urban yuppies flock to restaurants and bars to soak in the vibe of The Drive. The result being the once affordable neighbourhood has now become as expensive as other areas of the city with rents rising to market value and the price tags on homes sky rocketing. In spite of these changes the neighbourhood continues to attract a mosaic of people with alternative ideas and expressions; artists, poets, musicians, activists and urban gardeners to name a few. It's as if the neighbourhood is a living, breathing entity, a beast that cannot be tamed. It's a place where you can't help but sense it is okay to be who you want to be and to express whatever that is freely, whether that be sporting an Easter bunny costume in July, skateboarding down the street while playing guitar or holding a demonstration for the rights of those whose voices are not always heard.

In my early days in Vancouver I was struck by the amount of people who were homeless and in great need of services that seemed not to be available. I had experienced living in a third world country and wondered why it was in a country as rich as Canada there is so much poverty and despair. It was indeed heartbreaking and finding some way to be a part of a solution beyond handing out money played continuously with my conscience.

One particular cold November evening stands out for me. I had not been in the city very long but was already beginning to build up some emotional calluses to deal with the suffering I was seeing on the streets on a daily basis. November is never an easy month for any of us, it gets dark at 5pm, it rains and it rains and it's cold and did I mention it rains. On this evening I was hitting an all-time low. I was getting clearer about what I wanted to be doing, but no clearer about how I would get there. To cut the story short, I was having a spectacular pity party for one. So to try and switch gears I decided to take myself to a movie. I was running late and moving quickly; I had forgotten my umbrella and was using my super powers to walk between the rain drops (It wasn't working). As I was nearing the Commercial and Broadway Skytrain station I could hear this man yelling, "Can someone please help me" followed by much swearing. I took a breath and said to myself, I can't deal with this tonight. I could see that people were not only ignoring him but crossing the street to avoid him. I was about to join in this parade when that same nagging voice that brought me to Vancouver said, "just go ask him if he is okay".

I approached with caution, and it did not take long for me to move beyond his large stature and tough street persona of tattoos and piercings to see that he was simply a boy, alone and scared with no one to care about him accept for his German Sheppard companion. When I said the words, "are you okay?" he replied "have you ever been so hungry you are just mad?" I said yes, in fact I recognize that feeling. I gave him some money to go get a slice of pizza. Dan told me he had just arrived in Vancouver and that no one would talk to him or help him. I suggested he may want to work on his approach as he was actually scaring people. He managed to laugh a bit. He told me that he didn't want to do anything bad but that he was thinking about it to get money for food. We talked about his dog and it was clear that even though Dan was starving and desperate that the dog was the one thing keeping him from a path of complete self-destruction. And, for the record, Dan made sure the dog had food when he did not.

I walked away feeling grateful for the connection but once again feeling that I wish there was some way that I could do more to address the issue of homelessness in my community. And the next day as I was walking down Commercial Drive I literally saw a sign for 'The Under One Umbrella Homeless Connect Event' to be held in January. I called the number and signed up to volunteer.

A few weeks after meeting Dan, I saw him again. He was much happier as he had connected with some other street youth in the area; he, like me, had found a sense of community on The Drive. I took him to buy some fries and was pleased to be able to tell him about the upcoming Homeless Connect event that could help him to connect to services he was in need of.

I continue to volunteer with UOU and live in the neighbourhood. I am often challenged at times to remember a pearl of wisdom once given to me; to always choose connection over disconnection. My question, "what can I do" lingers, as it meets the ever increasing complexity of homelessness. But all that angst disappears when I simply allow myself to see whoever it is that crosses my path and to allow them to see me. It is in this recognition of others that the humanity within me is allowed to blossom. It's as if for a moment I get to be a magician as the invisible now becomes the visible.

Vancouver Aboriginal Transformative Justice Services Society

The Vancouver Aboriginal Transformative Justice Service Society (VATJSS) is a non-profit agency that provides restorative justice, youth outreach and homelessness outreach services to aboriginal people within the Metro-Vancouver area.

The restorative justice service provides offenders and victims with satisfying and culturally appropriate alternatives to the mainstream criminal justice system. The services are a non-adversarial, non-retributive approach to justice that emphasizes healing in victims, meaningful accountability of offenders, and the involvement of community members in creating a healthier and safer community.

The main objectives of the VATJSS program are to offer a restorative justice process which focuses on repairing the relationships among those affected by crime, the victim, the offender, their families and the community, while empowering individuals to formulate appropriate responses and strategies to deal with the crime and to directly participate in processes affecting the overall well being of the community. To accomplish these objectives, the VATJSS utilizes a Community Council forum made up of volunteers, an Elder, the victim and offender and their support people to facilitate the discussion of the offence, its effects, and the causes of the behaviour that led to the offence. At the conclusion of the forum, a healing plan is developed with a goal towards making amends and positively reintegrating the victim and offender into the community.

The Homelessness Initiative assists individuals and families who are homeless, or at risk of becoming homeless, in maintaining or finding housing within the community. The program also provides services such as referrals to other connections that they may need in their life (eg., counselling, food, clothing, furniture, income tax, etc.).

The Youth Outreach Program provides culturally appropriate life-skill workshops and family interventions for aboriginal youth who are at-risk of homelessness in order to broaden their personal development and address the risk factors of aboriginal youth in the Metro Vancouver area. VATJSS is located at 107-1602 East Hastings Street in Vancouver.

On The Drive
Two Weeks

I am someone who tends to stay very close to home, and home is Main and Hastings. I get lost easy and I'm a creature of habit. Take me out of my own environment and I will struggle to meet basic daily needs.

One time, by accident, due to being too fucked up to know any better, I ended up on Commercial Drive. I was too paranoid to take a bus or Skytrain home and I had no idea how I'd gotten to Commercial Drive in the first place. Of course I had no money on me and I was in no shape to make any. I could tell this area was not much different than Hastings as far as homelessness and drug dealers were concerned, but the difference lay in the lack of community centres. On a good note, cigarette butts were lying everywhere. I collected butts and it kept me busy for a while. I tried to get them in a nonchalant manner without looking too obvious about what I was doing.

I remember sitting down at the McDonald's and someone handing me a cup of coffee. I smiled at the man who said he only bought it to use their bathroom, and that gave me the idea to show the coffee cup and ask for the bathroom to be unlocked. It worked, and I was relieved, literally.

Still not too sure where home was, I began roaming alleys, looking for bottles, expecting to find a bottle depot along the way. Much to my surprise, Safeway was the only place to cash in bottles that I could find, and they only took a limited quantity. I did manage to talk and whine my way to a $4.80 cash-in, pleading ignorance and poverty.

Any sane person would have used the money to get home. I on the other hand used it to buy more crystal meth and began walking, merely hoping to stumble my way back home. I walked all night, collected more bottles, and be damned if I didn't end up right back on Commercial Drive again. Good thing I wasn't wired to methadone back then like I am now, or it would have been much worse, or maybe I would have tried harder to get home. As it was it took me two weeks to make my way back to Main and Hastings. During that time I got to know the area a bit, learned how to do some fine dining out of a garbage bin, and smoked my brains out until I ran out of rolling papers. I finally straightened out one day enough to get on the Skytrain and got my ass home. I can't say my memories of the neighbourhood are fond, but they're memories still the same.

MELANIE KONKIN

1582 William Street

Destination: Vancouver

Arrival: August 2006

Neighbourhood: Commercial Drive

Purpose: Reconnection to self

When the idea of moving to Vancouver presented itself I said "Why not?" I packed up my stuff, my two dogs got in the car, and I started the long five-day drive across Canada. The neighbourhood I landed in was Commercial Drive, which was chosen deliberately for its cultural diversity and artistic spirit. What better place to rediscover the person I had lost? Surely amongst all this inspiration the real me would leap at the chance to re-emerge? But it wasn't that easy.

The house, located at 1582 William Street, a tiny blue and white cottage house that freakishly often attracted a most eclectic group of people; the young couple and their golden lab who preferred to do his business on my lawn; the girl who had emotional tantrums outside my front window; the fire hula-hoop sister who practiced her craft daily yet couldn't avoid burning herself; the older Chinese women with wide-brimmed hats and sour smiles picking through the recycling box; the young boys playing lacrosse on bikes in the park; the random musicians, jugglers and transient folks in the park, all serving to entertain and enlighten me, yet the me I was patiently waiting for still remained quiet.

Every day I would wake-up, jump in the car and drive to work. Work consisted of standing in line at Starbucks, sitting in a grey on grey cubicle, attending countless meaningless meetings where nothing ever got accomplished and pretending to care about a co-worker's new set of baby pictures, "Oh, look at that, she's peeing all by herself."

I lived in this cool, vibrant neighbourhood and yet the major part of my day was drab and lifeless.

I never did find myself while living on The Drive. That's a road I keep travelling but I do keep fond memories of the neighbourhood and our tiny blue house. Like the first time I ordered the Portobello mushroom burger at Stella's and never realized it wasn't meat, or the time we sat and watched people dancing in the park each only tuned into music on their own iPods, or the time our water system backed up and I found myself in the shower with the remnants of our feta, spinach pasta dinner floating by my feet and quickly realized that the kitchen and bathroom shared the same water line, or the time they put up a huge screen in the park primarily made of bed sheets and a live band re-enacted Metropolis, or saving all my good recyclables for Jean (she was scrawny with a bad limp and a wrinkled-up face that crackled into a thousand bits each time she smiled) or Cafe Calabria, the place where Italy threw up all over itself but, man, the espresso is good and the people watching even better.

The Drive will always be my landing to Vancouver and in many respects the place where I gained the courage to dream of another way.

ADRIENNE FOSTER

Remembrance Day

They walk by in ones and twos; some with babies in carriers on their back, all headed in the same direction. Some hold big plaid umbrellas. Some have hoods pulled over their head. Some wear baseball caps or knitted toques. There are children with their parents, teenagers, middle age folks, and elderly people. It is a steady stream of people out in the cold drizzle that sporadically turns into a downpour.

I am watching the informal march from the coziness of the café with a big picture window. Around me there is the buzz of the espresso maker and the hubbub of four conversations going on at once drowning out the football game on the big screen TV on the back wall.

At 10:50 am I pack up my belongings and head down the street. There must be 500 people standing in the muddy grass and along the sidewalks at the cenotaph in Grandview Park. Two rows in front of me I see a toddler in a neon yellow rain suit wearing white and blue boots and a green helmet covering the yellow hood. His hands are red from the cold but he doesn't seem to care as he squashes the mud puddles. Close by his father watches over him.

At 11 am everyone is silent and standing still. The sound of the lonely bugle rises above the sputtering drizzle. The crowd is respectful through the dull moan that must be the speeches even though most of us can't see or hear what is going on. The rain is getting more persistent.

As the cold and damp start to seep into my bones, it is hard not to look at my watch. After twenty minutes, the droning stops. Through the cracks in the swaying crowd I can see the people inside the yellow, taped off area form a line and start walking to the street. What caught my eye was not their age or dark rain gear, but their hats. Leading the parade are a dozen Veterans in deerstalker type hats each with a long feather affixed to the side. Next come a handful of men wearing black soggy caps that are festooned with a cascade of small, black feathers drooping down one side. And then they are gone. (November 11, 2008)

LINDA ROBERTS

The Card

I have lived in the neighbourhood for almost a decade. I love it here. I am a member of The Wall Street Community Garden and The Forgotten Triangle Group now known as the Under One Umbrella Society. In fact, my husband Damian is the coordinator of this story project commemorating Vancouver's 125 year Anniversary.

We both also had a shop on Hastings called The Art Garden. Unfortunately, we had to close after two years as the economy and, more importantly, people were suffering badly. However, it did bring in a lot of lovely people from our community and many wonderful conversations. In particular, a woman named 'Betty'. I know Betty from our community garden and she lives a stone's throw away from our home. She is frequently seen in the park across the street and at McDonald's having coffee and lively conversations with her partner 'Stan'.

Betty is one of the most well-read people I have ever met. She is also one of the most thoughtful. When we had our shop my mum fell very ill and she lives with my dad in Edmonton. She ended up having major surgeries and I visited her several times through this. Just before a trip to Edmonton, Betty came into the shop saying that she had heard my mum was ill and that I was going to Edmonton to be with her. She was so concerned and said that she would be thinking good thoughts for her. After my return, my mum was better. Since that time, three years ago, Betty has asked me first about my mum and then about me and Damian.

My birthday fell on a day while I was working at the shop. Betty came in and learned it was my birthday.

From that time on, I have received in the mail (the only one I get in the mail) a beautiful birthday card with a lovely message and a very interesting hand written letter. Interesting because Betty is bipolar, schizophrenic, has been hospitalized/institutionalized for long periods of time and lives on social assistance. She also has several physical health issues. She has confided in me about some very sad and very happy events in her life. I cherish the conversations I have with her and appreciate the effort she makes in sending me cards and letters (we don't do this enough anymore!). There are so many great stories of our neighbourhood that I can think of but when I had to decide on one, I knew it had to be about Betty. She represents the true beauty here. People caring about other people from many walks of life no matter what they may be suffering with or from.

There are several amazing non profits here too, like The Kettle Friendship Society, Watari, and Franklin House for Women. We live by the water and can see the Eagle's nest at the Port. We take our dog Ziggy on many walks here and he loves it too. Our building has many pets, artists and all-around nice people. I work 10 minutes away on the Downtown Eastside as a support worker for survival sex workers. People there are just as lovely and so inspiring. When I come home, I know I will continue to be around other people who care about people. Thanks to Betty and all the other beautiful people I have met, I am so proud to call Grandview Woodland my home!

ALKA MURPHY

Only on Commercial Drive

My story of the Grandview Woodland area must begin with my parents. My dad graduated from Britannia. His story is a typical Italian immigrant story with his parents coming over from Southern Italy and settling in East Van. My Mother graduated from Van Tech and met my father in grade 10. High school sweethearts. They tell me stories of going out on dates at Nick's Spaghetti House and dances at the Pender and Georgia Auditoriums as well as seeing shows like Ella Fitzgerald and Louis Armstrong at The Cave.

My mom and dad dated longer than they were married so there we parted ways, sending us as far from East Van as my mom could go - the west side.

After many years of living and growing up in all parts of Vancouver we all finally made our way east to Commercial Drive, back to where it all began. Actually, we couldn't have moved any closer to each other. My mom and younger sister lived on McSpadden. My older sister lived two houses down from them where she raised her two daughters. I was one street over on 4th Avenue. Not to mention aunts, uncles and cousins all living within walking distance. We have truly moved back home.

What I love about living ½ a block off The Drive is the feeling of community. My neighbours and I often gather outside our homes catching up, looking out for each other and trying to figure out who owns which cat. Yes, our street should be renamed Cat Alley.

I have seen many changes in this neighbourhood but the one thing that is constant is the vibrant energy of Commercial Drive. The best of food, entertainment and people gathering on the street. While I am talking about the people on the street I want to mention the gangs of older men that hang out in groups outside various coffee shops. I used to be offended that these men, old enough to be my grandfather, would ogle and whistle at me as I walked by. Now I have a totally different attitude. I think "good on them for keeping the sparkle in their eye and still, at their age, admiring a pretty girl." Perhaps they are still acting like they did as teenage boys hanging out on Commercial with all their friends. Better that than at home feeling lonely in front of the tube.

My mom has a vivid memory of going for her morning coffee at the Continental Café early one morning and seeing a young woman sitting at the outside table, coffee and cigarette in hand, wearing a long white wedding gown and high heel shoes with her hair in huge rollers.

Only on Commercial Drive.

SANDRA TAYLOR

DID YOU KNOW.... That Fourth Avenue used to be called Electric Avenue?

GW Community Policing Centre

The Grandview Woodland Community Policing Centre is a volunteer-driven non-profit organization that works in a partnership with the Vancouver Police Department and support from the City of Vancouver to promote crime prevention and safety through a range of programs, activities and services for residents, businesses, and agencies in the Grandview-Woodland neighbourhood. The GWCPC is dedicated to providing crime prevention assistance and education to the Commercial Drive corridor and surrounding area. We encourage, through education and engagement in volunteering with the GWCPC, all the members of the community to become active participants for increasing safety awareness and decreasing opportunities for crime to occur. The Grandview Woodland CPC regularly communicates to our community through our main publication, The News Beat, and we also offer access to important crime stats and local news.

In November 1994, the Britannia CPO opened in free space donated by the Britannia Community Centre. Two patrol officers were assigned by the VPD to work with the CPO. The Britannia CPO worked under the umbrella of the Britannia Community Centre. Their own Advisory Committee was set up through elections from the CPO's volunteer roster, which was over 100 strong in the early months of the CPO.

ML Burke worked with volunteers, the community, other CPOs, and the VPD to establish the CPO's core programs during the first year, after which part-time coordinators were hired to continue the work. Now the GWCPC is in its fourteenth year of operation, having consistently provided the Grandview Woodland community with service to both businesses and residents, all of whom are the core target of our service area in and around Commercial Drive. We have been operating out of our new location since 2004. We have made the office more community and VPD friendly. With more officers using our office for meals, research, and meetings, the GWCPC provides a more visible police presence in our neighbourhood.

Coffee to Go

The Commercial Drive festivities have always been fun. The Italians would make their sausages and sell soccer t-shirts. There would be at least one stage where a person was singing. The Commercial Drive stores would have their wares for sale on tables. I love being in a crowd and love the people. We always had sunny days for the festivities. Joe's Café would be selling coffee. At Joe's it is $1.75 per coffee and it tastes like cappuccino. You can have it in a coffee mug or a to-go mug. I like buying the coffee to go, and then going to Grandview Park and sitting there with a smoke, watching the children play. There are five people at Joe's Café, two Italians and the three that work for them. They are all nice people that are friendly and polite. They'll have the soccer on the big screen TV too. Joe's never seemed to have a problem with a patron and I like his coffee more than Starbucks'.

MARY SMITH

Photo courtesy of Ella Mae Lansdowne

Urban Native Youth Association

As Metro Vancouver's only Native youth program-providing organization, the Urban Native Youth Association (UNYA) works to empower Native youth through our 21 programs including education & training, personal support, live-in programs and sports & recreation. Our programs range in age from 13-29, but each program has its own age range.. Our work also includes community development, training, research, educational materials, and advocacy. Our main goal is to provide opportunities for Native youth that will help them reach their full potential and personal goals.

UNYA offered its first program to Native youth in 1988 and became a non-profit society in 1989. UNYA is also a federally registered charitable organization. UNYA's mandate is to provide meaningful opportunities for Native youth (including aboriginal, Métis, Inuit, First Nations, status, and non-status) in the urban setting. Our goal is to be a safe place for Native youth to come and find out about programs and services at UNYA and in the broader community. As of 2011, we have over twenty programs, over one hundred volunteers, almost 100 full and part-time staff, and 200+ community partners. UNYA's annual operating budget is approximately $4.5 million.

Today, approximately 60% of the Native population lives in urban settings, and 60% of the overall Native population is under the age of 25. UNYA continues to focus on prevention because we believe that Native youth lack opportunity, not ability. We also believe that Native youth have the right to live safe, healthy, and positive lives that are free from negative influences. UNYA strives to address issues that negatively affect the lives of Native youth by providing a supportive continuum of care, with a large focus on prevention-based activities such as peer leadership, sports and recreational activities, and health programs. We strive to meet their immediate and long-term needs. When they have access to opportunities, our children and youth excel, and they have many strengths to build upon. Should youth become involved in street or negative lifestyles, we're also here to support and help them make positive changes in their lives. UNYA will continue to adapt to meet the changing needs of today's Native youth to ensure that they have the best chance possible to lead safe, healthy, and positive lives.

Youth are consulted in the development of new UNYA programs and services, as we feel youth are the experts in their own lives and are in the best position to advise us on youth issues. UNYA always strives to have at least four Native youth on our board of nine members. Youth board members, in particular, have been very helpful in ensuring that UNYA remains youth focused, that youth voice is heard and responded to throughout the organization, that new programs are relevant to Native youth, and that youth needs are being positively addressed. UNYA's Board members are committed to being active mentors and learners so that their Board term can be a fulfilling learning experience that will increase their skills and knowledge. We also actively seek to engage Native youth as staff members, in practicum positions, as summer students, and in training opportunities. Youth are influential in programming through the direct input they provide as participants, through surveys and community meetings, in user group consultations for the new Native Youth Centre, and ongoing research and community development initiatives.

UNYA continues to focus much of our efforts on community development initiatives, for we believe that the strengthening of our community as a whole can have a tremendous and positive impact on the lives of Native youth. Over the years, UNYA has strived to contribute to the positive development of our community by creating our Full Circle and Helping Hands manuals. Other recent initiatives included the creation of several new resources for youth, including a new Health Booklet, Health-promotion posters, and a cookbook, Eating Healthy on a Budget. We continue to host community meetings and forums, offer training on youth issues to the community, serve on community steering committees, attend consultation meetings, conduct research, develop innovative programs, hire and train youth, participate on the Metro Vancouver Aboriginal Executive Council, and create a wide range of partnerships as part of our efforts to strengthen and expand services for Native youth.

For many years, UNYA has been working to develop a new Native Youth Centre at Commercial & Hastings in the eastside of Vancouver. Youth have been involved throughout this process on the Building Advisory Committee, the Design Committee, and on the Capital Campaign Committee. Youth have also been involved in developing the Permanent Donor Recognition program, developing marketing materials and the project logo, meeting with funders, and participating in focus groups, a community meeting, and on user groups during the facility program stages. We also welcome community support and donations which will help us make the Native Youth Centre a reality.

GRANDVIEW WOODLAND IS AWESOME BECAUSE…

...this is a real community. People know their neighbours - the neighbours that live in the house next door and the neighbours who are homeless. Not in every case, of course, but there is a real sense that people are looking out for each other in this neighbourhood.
(Tanya)

Sorry Mister, You Have to Move

Winter came early to Grandview Woodland at the close of 2010 with a rare November dump of snow and a chilly wind that smothered overnight the lush rain forest landscape of our neighbourhood with a cold icy blanket.

We still don't have a permanent shelter in our 'hood so when the cold comes in and you're sleeping rough you'd rather suffer the elements and stay put than risk getting rolled in unfamiliar territory.

For "Jean-Paul" that meant holing up and waiting it out in an unused covered doorway of a local business in the light industrial zone near Clark and Hastings.

Jean-Paul is a homeless guy living in and off the streets of Grandview Woodland. From back east originally he settled in Vancouver some time ago. He is a self-proclaimed "rocker", completely devoted and unrepentant to his addiction to crack and untiring in his efforts to make a few bucks to get what he needs. He mules dope, bins for discarded treasures, and vends what he can to whomever he can. But he doesn't panhandle. He's made that very clear. I know him from work.

I'm an outreach worker. I live down by the port at the North end of GW. I spend most of my working days, these days, talking to guys like Jean-Paul. I have stuff to give and time to listen. And if you want to come in from living outside I just might be able to find what you're looking for.

The first time I accompanied Jean-Paul to check out a place the previous March he told me that most people thought he was hopeless, housing-resistant, no landlord would give him a look, expectations too high (a room with a toilet and bath). I begged to differ.

I went with him to one of the few hotels not on the DTES; another condition of Jean-Paul's. The room was small, 10x10, moldy wood smell, an old cracked porcelain sink, just a hot plate to cook on and a thin metal framed bed that took up half the space. Shared showers and toilets in the common hall. $475 a month. $100 bucks over the allowance given by the Ministry for shelter.

And then there were the rules. Jean-Paul started nodding off as John the manager read the house rules from a yellowed laminated card. "No guests after 10 p.m.".

Jean-Paul started swaying slowly left to right. He struggled to keep his chin up.

"You've got a ground floor room but I don't want to see anyone coming in through the window...we've got cameras you see..."

Jean-Paul's arms were lifting slightly as if reaching out. His eyes were mostly closed. Watching his head bob up and down, his body sway yet remain standing, was hypnotic. "Don' worry I'm a good guy, just wanna a place to crash", he got out.

"OK, get the intent to rent approved," John the Manager says, "and you can move in today."

Jean-Paul took it and gave it a good show but he lasted less than a week.

Sometimes, I think he took the room just for me; I was working so hard to get him a place inside.

Or maybe not. Jean-Paul disclosed that the manager reminded him of someone from his past who was supposed to be there when something had happened, but wasn't. Wasn't there. Besides, the hotel's location far from Grandview Woodland was way out of his comfort zone. And too many rules...

I didn't see Jean-Paul around much after he ditched the SRO. He was either laying low and spending time in Hastings Sunrise or had gone out west like a lot of outdoor folks do during the warm months.

He showed up again in the neighbourhood in early gall, I met him dumpster diving behind the Safeway on 10th. He asked me again if there might be a bachelor available in the area, in his price range, with its own bathroom. A place he could call home. I said I'd look around.

After that reunion he started coming by the office now and then. Or I'd see him early in the mornings when I was doing outreach in the lanes and parks.

Jean-Paul finally settled in the doorway of a nearby business which was good 'cuz I knew where to find him and could pass on messages or drop stuff off. When that November blast of snow came I got worried about him so I brought over some blankets and other gear to help keep him warm.

It was dark and freezing the morning after the snow fell and I begged him to consider going to a shelter, at least until the storm passed. He refused. I said I would check up on him, and I did, several times a day. By the end of the first day he looked like a popsicle, huddled up to the chin in every piece of clothing he had.

I let the folks at the community policing centre know about his situation and asked if they could pass a message to the police on the night shift to check in on him.

The next morning was still cold and snowy and when I got to his spot it was hard to tell if he was even there, just a pile of stuff. I could see he had been visited during the night. There was a brand new thick blanket all rolled up, a heavy winter coat and a large soup and coffee from Timmy's sitting on top of his meager possessions. But when I lifted a corner of his sleeping bag Jean-Paul was gone.

I asked around and checked his usual spots and kept coming back to the doorway. More clothes and food had been left for him but he did not return. I asked the police if they had picked him up. They hadn't. I called around to the local hospitals. No-one had seen him. After a few days it became clear that he had vanished without a trace.

A few weeks passed into December and work became busy. Christmas is a hard time for the homeless. Jean-Paul was always in the back of my mind. On a hunch, I called the Ministry to see if he had picked up his Christmas supplement. Every single person on welfare gets a $35 allowance for the giving season. My contact informed me that he had in fact picked up his cheque. He was gone but he was alive. And I was relieved.

I saw Jean-Paul again the following April 2011. I bumped into him at the recycling depot and he gave me a big hug. A huge grin on his face.

"Jean-Paul" I said, "where have you have been? It's been so long since we've seen you around."

"I got what I wanted, "he said. " My own place with my own bathroom! Only $375."

I couldn't believe it. Turned out he'd abandoned his spot the first night the storm hit. He'd managed to get into one of the temporary winter shelters and from there had been offered a room when the shelter closed the following spring.

His new home is far from perfect but it is close enough to Grandview Woodland to make him happy and I now see him about regularly doing his thing.

No one else took his spot in that doorway.

The owners of the business had put up a sign; "Sorry Mister, you have to move, we are going to be using this doorway. Thanks for understanding."

DAMIAN MURPHY

Photo courtesy of Kelliey Montgomery

Wild and Free

I am going to talk about a memory of my children and the first time they crawled. I heard from their foster caregiver after they got their last shot from the doctors that my kids had started to crawling. The first time they were crawling they got on their hands and knees and were cruising around wild and free! We brought them to the park and put them on the swing. I got to push them on the swing and take them on the slide. That is where they got their pictures taken with me. After the swings they went onto the grass so they could crawl some more, it was so fun to watch them crawl on the grass, I got my second picture with them there. We took a walk with the boys around the block, let them roam around and played around with them for a bit. It was a great memory.

FRANCIS

Photo courtesy of Ella Mae Lansdowne

Waiting for the Sun: THE AWAKENING

Hello sunshine, you who brings her radiance to the day and light to the night. The moon, that cold dark sphere, without your reflection upon its heart; its body; its mind. It waits for you with a patience like a howling dog longing for its owner, while you shine on the earth; waiting, waiting for oh that night, to catch but a glimpse, a mere taste of your might, only to helplessly watch as your light turns to the mother and oh he waits until again he feels your loving embrace trickle over his bareness; his lack of life. Ah the lamenting of the moon, despairs all day and filled with your limelight by night. You are his saving grace, his reason; his compassionate kiss that he should always dread and yet is in want of until again you bring life back into his eyes with your always present radiant glow.

Ah to be chased by the sun, too bad the moon's plight; to be chased by the sun with no chance of its true embrace; of no more than a taste. What a full the moon would have been to hope to hold onto the sun; she who can melt the sea with but a passing glimpse. No, that wise old man in the night, who is always at her mercy, knew to shadow himself from her body of all light from time to time lest he be whirled into tears with no comfort in his sight. Though, if he could, he would let himself fall inside of her warmth to be consumed in her light...but then who would shine in the night? No, the moon, that old wise man cared too much for his mother to leave her side. He would sacrifice his only chance at love with another to keep her tears inside.

Ah the sadness of the moon, his poor lamented eyes; always gazing; always longing for the sun to brighten up his night. But his sadness is not forever; only while his sunshine is gone; his only saving grace is knowing that she won't be gone too long. His only source of joy is hearing mother as she sings her song all the day long, long, dong a bing, bing, bong, bong, bong, the beating of his heart goes on and on and on. Was he really so wise to live in wait of her loving embrace; or just another fool, paralysed by her lovely face? Who knows what the story knows, but the author, the master; the master of fate?

Where has everyone gone? Oh yes, to the warmth of their homes, and it is not they who have left, but I who am now out in the cold; it is I who now must face alone the night. Armed with a sleeping bag, stuffies, and shopping cart, I roam the streets looking for somewhere to crash out that's dry. I am lucky if I have liquor to quell the utter loneliness. My stuffed animal companions develop personalities and we become best friends. They always ride in the front of my shopping cart so that I know I haven't lost them too. I find a place to lie down and lay out my bed, stuffies too. Not too long afterwards I cover my head for the night; the tears begin to flow. I hold my stuffies tight as if they are my friends, children, or lovers. I dare not lose these to this misery I have made to mine own end. I am so alone and scared, it seemed that no-one cared, not my friends or family, now not blaming, I see what I have done and punish myself with more thoughts toward despair. I had traded my friends, family and lovers for alcohol's sake and worse demons still, whose peddlers, danced up and down the street, offering what they had to any who passed them by whose sinister smile reeked of human bile. Their hands held out begged you to submit to their desire, (human souls bathing in fire).

I woke the next morning amazed that I was not dead, in fact I was quite cozy within my sidewalk blanket bed, cozy that is until I rolled out of my blanket's warmth, then the cold was real again. I was always pleasantly surprised upon waking that no harm had come to me, never mind the reassurance of more booze when I'd see that my cart of bottles had gone the night without winning over any thief's heart's desire. Sometimes I even found that money or food *had been neatly placed somewhere in plain sight, while I had slept. I always felt blessings on mornings like those. It was these gifts in the night that restored my faith in humanity, that there was indeed still good in their heart of hearts. Surely, I thought, that if strangers see here a man worth saving, then perhaps I am not yet dead to the master maker (God). Surely this meant I still have some purpose that I have yet to invent. It seemed, that all alone and with nowhere else to turn, that God himself or perhaps his elect, had been sent with rich blessings for this man who was not yet spent. By design, these wonders that I would find along my road seemed made specific and only for my sake, not possibly for another. By what seemed quite magical, I always seemed to find just what I needed and mostly even more than I could carry without strain. It was then, I suppose, that I learned how to share. Yes, it seemed I always had enough to stay alive, both in body and in mind. Through all this suffering I would be made to see the light had not died. I had simply been stone drunk blind.*

Soon I would realize that it is from here, (homelessness), that a man learns to be a man or worse damnations are sure to follow. It is from here, (poverty), that a man learns to share what he has for its own sake. It is from here, (irresponsibility), that I learned what I'd let no human teach; how to love the land as thyself. I found myself cleaning messes in the alleyways for the sake that such should not be in anyone's eyes. No-one that lives in the neighbourhood deserves to see such a sight, let alone be expected to clean it too. No, that should be my gift to the land and man as well, for it was the land that I now fed from and the people who dwell there that deposit their waste from which I could feed. Blessings that followed, (and there have been many), compelled me to be helpful and honest in my ways; to always do what I can. Imagine that, a homeless wreck of a man can still learn how to stand.

Photo courtesy of Ella Mae Lansdowne

An Everlasting Camping Trip

It's about 4:30 pm on a Tuesday afternoon and it's been a slow day, hopefully to pick up sometime soon. Where I sit and panhandle to sell and sleep on the Drive, I am known to different people as 'hats', 'coats' or 'pockets'. To others I am also known as 'the garden gnome' or 'the book guy at Third and Commercial'. As you can probably tell, I am a homeless person. I have been asked what I think it's like to be homeless, and I say it's like an everlasting camping trip, never to end, unless I want it to.

My real name is Richard Nuisker, and I wanted to write a bit about myself and tell you more about The Drive; it has its good and also its bad side. To start, I've been on and off the Drive for about 18 years and met some pretty interesting people along the way; some good and some bad, some cool and some hot-headed.

Whenever I've been asked if I saw a certain show or movie, I tell people I don't need to – I get all the excitement I want watching the drama and the soap opera on Commercial Drive just by opening my eyes in the morning right up until I close my eyes at night.

That brings me to a winter when I stayed at Commercial and Third. I was shoveling snow on the sidewalk when I notice a guy buying a lot of salt. I stopped shoveling and sat down to have a smoke break and the same guy walked by again. He must have been carrying at least 6 or 7 more bags of salt. I just had to ask him what he was doing. He replied he was trying to get his truck out from being stuck in the snow and ice. I asked if I could help dig him out with the shovel that I had, so my buddy and I went with him to help. After two hours of work in freezing weather we were all cold and tired but still had not been able to get his truck dug out, so I went on my way back to my spot to sleep and get warm. He did come back the next day to say thanks and let me know he eventually got his truck out. Ever since then he's been a friend.

Oh no, I can't forget about the things that have also happened to me while selling my books, knickknacks and other miscellaneous things on the street over the years; like having one person come along and buy everything I had to sell in one shot, or leaving my spot when I've packed up only to come back just to find someone else has come along and stolen everything and what's left is strewn all over the place for me to clean up again and again; or the other people that set up beside me just to leave me their garbage to throw away. Sometimes whatever BS comes my way makes me just want to explode like an erupting volcano but having my cool-headed, laid-back ways keeps me contained.

I remember two years ago I sat at my spot 24/7 and I made nothing from panhandling and selling for three solid weeks. Until one morning I woke up and a guy came by, opened his wallet and gave me $100 dollars not once, but twice. It was very kind thing to do and I have to say it was shocking to me. I held onto that one hundred dollar bill thinking the worst; wondering if it was a fake or if he had just robbed a store! To this day I still have not seen this person again to say thank you.

Thanks to that individual for the kindness he had to share with me and all the others who have given me change when they had so little to give; it's the thought that counts the most. I almost forgot for thank the people who've bought books from me and the businesses around me for letting me do the odd jobs, and errands that provided me with food and pocket change to get through the day.

In the end, it was all good.

THE GARDEN GNOME, RICHARD NUISKER

DID YOU KNOW…

The corner of Grandview Woodland bounded by Nanaimo, Hastings, Clark and the waterfront is often referred to as 'the forgotten triangle' because it was historically under-serviced. In the 1970s, a committee of local residents, operating under the federally funded Neighbourhood Improvement Project, began to redress this imbalance by installing mini-parks. Oxford Park, Cambridge Park and Meditation Park were all developed as part of this initiative.

And I Was Sorry Too

The movement in the shadows drew me in. He marched with impunity down the centre of the avenue pulling on car doors, pressing his crooked nose against the tempered glass, searching desperately for opportunity – spare change, scattered cds, a lap top carelessly forgotten on the back seat. I watched with the attentiveness of a canine as he approached the neighbour's sedan. He popped open the trunk and reached for the prize – a heavy metal box crammed with carpentry tools and a Dewalt skill saw. He crossed the road and disappeared into the camouflage afforded by the dark. I burst out the front door and gave chase but my prey had disappeared into the back alleys and hidden gardens of the neighbourhood. I stood at the crossroads of Seventh and Victoria and scanned the deserted streets for movement. I impulsively headed north and when I reached McSpadden Park I decided that the thief might have cut across this grassy expanse. And there he rested in full view, his breath laboured, sitting on the edge of the street curb, the stolen bounty at his feet. " What the fuck are you doing?" he snarled as I approached. Given his compromised position, I was somewhat confident that I could snatch the box of tools without taking a punch or kick or the blade of a knife. As I reached for the metal handle, I saw his thin frame crumble under the weight of misery and self-loathing. He was sobbing. Through tears and yellow mucus and open sores he said he was sorry. Sorry for his crimes. Sorry for his out of control addiction. Sorry for the damage done. And I was sorry too.

CONNOR MURPHY

DID YOU KNOW…

The multi-purpose room at Templeton Pool boasts a sprung floor, just like the famous Commodore Ballroom. The running track at the same facility is built on a slight incline.

We are All Characters; Life, too

Incense wafting on a quiet Sunday afternoon. The heat reminds me of childhood in Malaysia, where it was not a fun thing to sweat in a sticky pinafore, carrying a heavy bag home on dusty paths. What Vancouver has given me is a more explicit sense of the seasonal. I had lived in Mt. Pleasant before I moved to the Drive. They say the Drive is not what it used to be but then which place is?

It's a neighbourhood for me, the one I come home to every day. I enjoy the weekend cellist; how she loves her burnt-red instrument; how we love her music outside Britannia.

I commute to work in a suburb. I have grown to like its green patches; not least of which is my gardener friend who gave me savory to smell, to hold, and to share when I ask him questions about plants and planting. I also enjoy the sound of the stream that runs in the neighbourhood; it reminds me that there is always a state of being. Sometimes I visualize communing with Elizabeth in her Garden of the Blind (Michael Ondaatje's In the Skin of a Lion).

Some work days are longer than others and there might be a slightly heavy feeling. But when the train pulls into Commercial station with its concrete embankment full of off-white morning glory, the congested feeling falls away. That must mean some sense of embodied demarcation, some sense of home; all the more welcome for it is quiet and unadorned.

When I was younger, it was not complete yet what a sense of home really means. I think the young are very busy, and so was I - in that young way; almost as if we have to be. I am still quite busy as I complete my fifth decade but it is different.

Last month I helped an elderly person for a bit as he made his way to the Skytrain elevator with his walker. Somehow we got chatting even though it had been a long workday for me. He told me about working for CN and about the places he had been. I shared some travel stories as well. He said he was from England years ago. He asked me where I was from. When I said Malaysia, he was clearly delighted and said, "The Malaysians I have met are very bright but they have been slapped around," to which I chuckled for,

1. no one can argue with the first part which is a very generous compliment, and

2: it was amazing, and it was grace, not to have to explain history.

We parted after half an hour of lively conversation, noting that we may meet again at that Translink platform. And I did something I don't usually do, I kissed someone I had just met on the cheek. I think that's what all the Edward Hopper individuals would have liked to do, in the right circumstances. The gentleman I made a connection with, or he with me, is almost a centenarian; he mentioned that he is 95, and that he is old. I took another look at him and said most truthfully, "Sir, you will always also be boyish," to which he chuckled. And that is how it is, when we are past our fifth decade, the girl or boy in us manifests very clearly again alongside the sum of our experience, or the dignity that has accrued.

SOOK KONG

PeaceMeal at Trout Lake

My sister-in-law, Alice Omengan-Claver, died in a hail of bullets in August 2006 in the Philippines. She was among thousands who were felled by the government's vicious attack against human rights activists and social justice advocates. A year later we were joined here in Canada by her widowed husband, Dr. Chandu Claver, the real target of the assassins who is now a political refugee, and his three kids.

On the fifth anniversary of Alice's death, Chandu and I exchanged e-mails about honouring the memory of his wife. He suggested that the day be a celebration of the lives and deeds of our kin, friends and colleagues who were slain, disappeared, or detained. This I thought was a grand idea. Having just come from a picnic for Gaza with Beth, a co-member in the Canada-Philippines Solidarity for Human Rights Committee, a picnic appealed as an attractive form of mobilizing and asking people to take action. It was fun and, coupled with art making, creative and participatory. My nephew, Diego, who used to live right next to Trout Lake, came up with a brilliant idea of turning picnic mats into canvases. "Why not add an exhibit of photos and the countless songs and poems that were written and dedicated to those whose lives were stolen?" I thought. And what better name to call it than PeaceMeal: A Picnic for Human Rights?

After a few weeks of fired-up meetings and preparations with Beth and Diego, and a flurry of emails, we were set. Diego, the computer whiz, put up the PeaceMeal website and we fanned out invitations. We had the perfect picturesque spot for our picnic: Trout Lake with its shady trees and welcoming expanse of green grass. To top it all off, it had a gazebo to shelter us in case of rain.

The night before our picnic, the sky was starless; the weather forecast said rain showers. My anxiety was appeased by the thought of the gazebo. We HAD to get that gazebo. The day of the picnic, I took a cab to the park. When the taxi driver learned that I was there for a picnic, he was incredulous. "At this time of the day?!" I was at the park with a handful of early morning joggers and half- awake, coffee-toting park habitués. The sky was leaden but I was nonetheless delighted to find the gazebo deserted, though full of trash and pigeon poop. Who cares? We had the venue to ourselves, or so I thought. Just as I finished reading the reservation sign overhead, a man carrying a huge red silk banner was approaching. Uh-oh. He did not look like Leo, a member of the migrant workers' group, who I was expecting to come. The man smiled and spoke in what sounded to me like Mandarin. Realizing that I was not Chinese, he just as soon shifted to English, his whole point being that they reserved the place a year ago. They were having their annual activity in the gazebo. My mind was whirring. There was not a dot of blue sky. Hmmm... A fight, flight, or freeze moment. I calmed myself. I had no choice but to remove all the RESERVED signs that I put on each poop-covered picnic table. We were both eyeing all the other tables scattered around. Don't be greedy, old man, I thought to myself. I walked past him and claimed three empty tables under the trees. I felt tiny drops fall on my arms. Why did we fail to check the reservation guidelines? It felt like an epic blunder.

I roused Jane, a member of Migrante BC, and broke the most unexpected news. Okay, so we were expecting rain, but not to be booted out of the venue by a reservation-wielding man boasting a guest list of 500 Chinese-Canadians. Jane promised to come at once with a tent. I knew Jane was one of the most dependable, resourceful and collected people one could work with.

I was mighty happy to see Beth arrive. She saw a trio of trees whose leafy branches formed a canopy that could repel a gentle shower. We were later joined by Mildred, a young community activist, and Diego. The set-up was punctuated with banter, high spirits, and an unusually heavy dose of prayer for sun. Please, no rain to soak the canvases and bleed the printed photographs.

Soon after, people came in steady trickles and our gallery under the trees was a-buzz with conversations. Passersby came and were astonished to learn that people working for social justice were being slaughtered or abducted in the Philippines. Our invitees came, bringing with them food, stories, and a palpable spirit of solidarity. Friends from Amnesty International, Spartacus Bookstore, Mobilization Against War and Occupation, Crafts for a Cause, Solidarity Labour Notes Choir, the Iranian Centre for Peace and Democracy and several members of the Mexican-Canadian community came. Members of Filipino-Canadian organizations were there. So were local artists, live-in caregivers, teachers, and members of the LGBT community. Guests readily signed the postcards addressed to the Philippine president, asking for the immediate surfacing of James Balao, the indigenous activist forcibly taken by state security forces. The petition for the release of political prisoners was passed around and signed. At any point in time during the picnic, people were busy drawing on the canvases or colouring the black and white images of the slain and the disappeared. The coloured images of Alice, students Karen Empeno and Sherlyn Cadapan, botanist Leonard Co, agriculturist Jonas Burgos, and detained poet Ericson Acosta danced in the wind as members of the Kathara Collective beat on their djembes and brass gongs. We gathered in a circle to pray, to remember, and to celebrate them all. Until our PeaceMeal ended, the sun shone mightily and steadily.

A local TV program covered the event. The newscaster said that PeaceMeal was going to be an annual event. If that is to be, we will still hold it on the grounds of Trout Lake, with or without reservations, come rain or sunshine. And the next time around, it shall hopefully be a victory picnic for peace, justice, and human rights.

LINGLING MARANAN-CLAVER

Book Exchange

Neighbourhood

The Book Exchange is an innovative community book exchange which was launched July 9 in East Vancouver. The bookshelf sits on a post at the corner of Lakewood Drive and Charles Street in the Grandview Woodland neighbourhood. Eileen Mosca, an artist and partner at Arts Off Main, initiated the idea when she learned of similar book exchanges in Portland and one that hangs outside a home in Victoria.

"It's like a bookstore but with no charge," Mosca said.

How it works is that people can bring a couple books at a time, though not their entire library or anything like that, and put them in the bookshelf. Then, people can browse the shelf when they pass by and take out books that they want. If they so choose they can bring the books back and take new ones.

Eileen has been living in Grandview Woodland for 31 years and she's also a Block Watch captain. In order to start the exchange, she got together with another Block Watch captain, Susan Lockhart, and applied for a Neighbourhood Small Grant from the Vancouver Foundation. The Neighbourhood Small Grants program was started by the Vancouver Foundation in 1999. Last year, they funded approximately 425 projects, ranging from $50 to $500.

Eileen and Susan got $350 for their project and with that money, some neighbours built the shelf with a Plexiglas cover and Eileen painted it. The Book Exchange has been received well by the community, Eileen said, with children's books and cookbooks proving to be the most popular.

"I think this could go in any neighbourhood and each would do it their own way," she said. "It's wonderful how people are still so into reading, by sharing with each other, it's completely affordable, i.e. free, and it's a treat for the kids. How great would it be for low-income neighbourhoods to have a book box like this, just for kids?"

And the box is proving to be more than a book exchange, there is also a social aspect to it whereby people begin to know more about their neighbours. "It's a great way to create a community because people would stand around and talk about things," she said. "People are getting introduced to each other over looking at books." Since the box's inception, Eileen has also added a community notice board and a chalk board on either side of the bookshelf.

"Hopefully, it'll turn out to be a place where people can communicate with each other in different ways — right now, the kids have pretty much taken over the chalkboard with drawings and thank you notes," she said.

Graham Clark, 4, was the ribbon-cutter at the opening event. He and his family have picked up a couple of books already, including one about giraffes that he loves. "It's kind of fun to see what hidden treasures you find there," said his mother, Denise Clark. "It's very community-minded, which I think is very neat."

"There's a real increasing hunger and desire for a grassroots way of building neighbourhoods," Eileen said. "I think people are feeling disconnected and this project makes it simple for people to reconnect at a neighbourhood level."

SETH MAKINSON

MOSAIC

MOSAIC is a multilingual non-profit organization dedicated to addressing issues that affect immigrants and refugees in the course of their settlement and integration into Canadian society. MOSAIC's mandate is to support and to empower immigrant and refugee communities, helping them to address critical issues in their neighbourhoods and workplace.

Since its inception in 1976, MOSAIC has assisted new immigrants and refugees through its numerous multilingual services. MOSAIC's programs and services are constantly evolving and developing in response to the needs of the community. Our work is guided by our vision of equality, social justice, equal access, and democracy. Our tools are advocacy, public education, community development, coalition building, and bridging with the broader community.

Nearly four decades since its humble beginnings in 1972 MOSAIC has established itself as a vibrant and reputable organization serving immigrants and refugees in the Greater Vancouver area. MOSAIC resulted from the amalgamation of two organizations: Multilingual Social Services (MSS) and Language Aid for Ethnic Groups (LAEG). Both had developed in response to the growing awareness of the daily challenges faced by Vancouver and area's non-English-speaking residents.

When the Grandview Woodland interagency team saw a need to reach out to the area's many immigrants the YWCA sponsored a grant, Project Contact, to bridge the language and cultural barriers between non-English-speaking people and the community. That project evolved into the Multilingual Information Service and, as its focus shifted to linking non-English-speaking people with social-services agencies, it was renamed Multilingual Social Services.

Based in the Downtown Eastside, LAEG also started in 1972; four women of different ethnic backgrounds planned the project while reflecting on the difficulties each had in adjusting to Canadian society. The project, launched without any external help, provided information, referral, counselling, interpretation and home-visiting services to immigrants.

Both agencies struggled from grant to grant and, for a time, had no funding. As well, they had to overcome the initial resistance of social service professionals and ethnic people themselves. In April of 1976, acting on the request of the (then) Department of Manpower and Immigration, MSS and LAEG combined to form MOSAIC (Multilingual Orientation Service Association for Immigrant Communities) and incorporated as a non-profit society. This was followed by registration as a charity.

MOSAIC has blossomed into a $19.4 million organization with over 200 staff and 300 contractors. Services include interpretation, translation, English classes, employment programs, community outreach and development programs, family support programs and bilingual and family counselling.

In March 2006 MOSAIC kick-started its 30th anniversary celebrations with a visit from Canada's Governor General Michaëlle Jean. The festivities wrapped up in September with Festival MOSAIC, held in partnership with the Vancouver East Cultural Centre and funded by the Vancouver Foundation.

In 2008 MOSAIC embarked on the process of accreditation with the Commission on Accreditation of Rehabilitation Facilities (CARF); a parallel strategic planning process was initiated in 2009. In October 2010 MOSAIC programs and services were successfully accredited with CARF. With the participation of its board, senior management, staff and key community partners, the organization's new Vision, Mission, Values and Strategic Goals were developed and adopted. And in July, as part of a continuing initiative to facilitate dialogue between policymakers and communities, MOSAIC hosted a meeting between Federal Minister of Citizenship, Immigration and Multiculturalism Canada Jason Kenney and leaders and representatives from the immigrant, public and private sectors.

And My Laundry Does Too

I've lived in this neighbourhood for about 33 years. I remember arriving in 1977. I was on a trolley bus on Broadway in rain pouring hard enough that the bus started hydroplaning when it crossed Clark Drive.

Grandview Woodland is an awesome community because of the cross-section of people, including me. When my relatives come to Vancouver I get them to rise with the sun (or the rain) and take a ride to the city or a trip to the Skytrain. We go over to our local Dim Sum or to our favourite hang-out spot, Bonn Café at Nanaimo and Broadway.

People here look out for each other. One July, I fell asleep at the Luminaries Festival at Trout Lake and people sat down all around me and just hung out. We all got up the next morning and I treated them to breakfast at Bonn Café. I also love the Saturday morning bike group which meets at Chio's. That's a fun day of putting about with nice people. I love Grandview Woodland because I belong and my laundry does too.

LAURA BLAKE

GRANDVIEW WOODLAND IS AWESOME BECAUSE…

…I get to hang out in Grandview Park. Also, I was panhandling one time when some dudes gave me paper money.
(Jimmy)

No Sheep Allowed

I have loved East Van since I moved here seven years ago. I grew up here, went to school here, lived in foster care here and it was one of the best times of my life. I attended the Phoenix Alternative School and the teachers were always super cool to me. One teacher in particular took the time to teach us how to make barrista coffee so every day we had mocha lattes. It was awesome.

This neighbourhood is very clean and people are usually nice. It's safe for our children to play outside and in the parks. I love to hang out in Grandview Park.

People here are so community minded. I love all the festivals and marches and demonstrations, especially Z day. It's so meaningful on so many levels. We aren't afraid to speak our minds so this is one community that isn't full of sheep.

AMBER FLEA

Photo courtesy of Brian Collins

Welcome to the Neighbourhood

I was transferred to the A&Z tool rental store at Commercial Drive and Sixth Avenue, and started working in the Grandview Woodland neighbourhood in 1983. At the store I met all kinds of interesting people. I was intrigued with what kind of neighbourhood it was because most customers where locals. I had heard the Eastside was a tough place but I didn't see it that way.

It was a hot summer that year and after work I would walk up Commercial Drive and get a cold drink or eat in a restaurant. There were so many multicultural restaurants. I went to a different one each time, and what a taste bud awakening experience. I also wandered the side streets and admired the heritage, character, and Vancouver Special houses. I observed multicultural families in their front yards, in their garden, or sitting on the stoop. I thought, "what an interesting and colourful place"

I attended the Italian Days festivals on Commercial Drive, the Caribbean Festival, and the Public Dreams Illuminaires Lantern Festival at Trout Lake. There was a lively punk rock and alternative music scene. I went to gigs at the New York Theatre, The Legion, The Odd Fellows Hall, and The Cultch. There were so many friendly and welcoming people and new experiences. Certainly the most interesting and vibrant neighbourhood I have ever experienced, and never a dull moment.

The arts, music, culture, food and diverse people, drew me to the area. I was fascinated with the Grandview Woodland neighbourhood and moved in soon after discovering it. I have lived and loved here ever since.

BRIAN COLLINS

THE EPIC OF ELVIS

Hello, my name is Elvis. The things I like to do are go walking around during night time, enjoying the quietness and the view on hills, driving around with a few friends around Horseshoe bay, and also watching movies.

(Elvis)

The Kettle Friendship Society

On July 19, 1976, a group of 20 concerned individuals prepared a brief addressing the need to develop a support service for individuals who were or had been receiving psychiatric treatment in the community. Gathered in the living room of a home in Kitsilano, a group of volunteers decided to form a non-profit society to provide support services to people with mental health disabilities. One of the first tasks at hand was to come up with a name. While tea was being prepared, the members brainstormed shouting out ideas. "Kettle!" someone then yelled, to indicate that the water was boiling on the stove in the kitchen.

When all the ideas were gathered, the recorder read back the suggestions. Much to everyone's amusement, 'Kettle' made the list. But upon serious reflection the volunteers realized that perhaps a kettle was an appropriate image. In a culture where so much revolves around socializing with a cup of coffee or tea, it was an ideal symbol for what the society was all about. It was about friendship. It was about caring. It was about family belonging and sharing. It was unanimous. The Kettle Friendship Society was born!

The mandate of this group was to provide 'care' as a complement to existing treatment facilities by attempting to enrich lives, broaden personal and social horizons and encourage participation in community life. It was intended to offer a low-key, softly directed social, recreational and life-skills program. The contribution of literally hundreds of members, board of directors, staff, volunteers and community 'friends' nurtured this dream into a remarkable reality. The Kettle's mandate is to provide an open door drop-in. It provides services and support in the areas of housing, advocacy, employment, meals and approximately 15 weekly life-skill programs.

The incorporated purposes of the Society are:

To work with individuals who have been or are presently in psychiatric treatment in the community by providing a centre for socialization and assistance in coping with life skills

To promote an independent low-key, softly directed program on a consistent and regular basis, not as a treatment facility but as a complementary services to all other existing facilities

To provide housing services for individuals who have been or are presently in psychiatric treatment in the community

To operate as a charitable organization and to receive donations of cash, lands properties or otherwise towards such objects and to apply for all necessary grants in aid of said objects

To do everything incidental and necessary to promote and attain the foregoing objects

Our Mission is supporting people with mental illness to lead healthier lives. We provide housing, employment, advocacy and support services, raise awareness of mental health issues and break down barriers for people with mental illness, and promote inclusion of people living with mental illness in all aspects of society.

The Before Story

Howdy, my name is Carl. I'm from the Lil'wat nation (Mount Currie) I met my spouse Larissa in 2005. We've been together for 6 years, But this is the before story of being a parent ...

I grew up with two brothers and four sisters and at least twelve nieces and nephews. I grew up in the Chinatown area since I was born. Whenever I went to Strathcona School I passed this church and, every so often, I saw two large eagles perched on the highest cross which I found very spectacular. After those days I knew that, even in the city, there is always something very beautiful to be experienced. On the weekends I used to walk around the neighbourhood with my parents who helped me grow stronger and grow to ignore all the drugs in the area. All those little strolls turned into walks to the PNE, then farther to Boundary Road which then took on a life of its own. I've walked to where ever I wanted to get to ever since.

Photo courtesy of Kelley Montgomery

My New Family

Hello, my name is Larissa. I am from Nuxalk Nation in (Bella Coola). I was originally from up north but I moved down to Vancouver with my mother near the Broadway and Commercial area. This is a one of most special moments in my life when I found out I was going to finally become a mother.

When I was starting out in those first few months I found out a certain amount of responsibility came with it - I had to eat bananas, grapes, and I had to exercise, all forced upon me by my wonderful mother and spouse Carl. Nine months and eight days later, Kaila was born, February 16, 2011 at 9:01 a.m. Outdoor experiences with Kaila are quite an endeavour at times 'cause so many people comment about a couple of certain traits on her. Frequently her cute baby cheeks, her wonderfully long hair, and her attentive observance of complete strangers. Being a mother in this area helps me out so much with the traditional programming that is held at UNYA and other youth groups. Parenting group keeps me and my baby healthy and happy. This community is my home and it surely treats me that way.

LARISSA

Photo courtesy of Kelley Montgomery

A Little Bit of Me

I first started falling in love with this area when I started going out in the community and just walking. Commercial Drive is so accepting of culture, uniqueness, individuality, race, political views, music, and pride. People in this neighbourhood just understand others a great deal better than most people in the Lower Mainland. When justice needs to be done in politics there are protests! When someone is hurt or needs help someone tries to do something about it. When I want to practise my spirituality I can. When Templeton Secondary has a school play people support their school. There are just so many people here who want to help and be involved. This is an involved community. Youth voices are heard! Adults are starting to understand their younger ones with restraint rather than ball-and-chaining them. This is my community and, as a Native person living in an urban setting, the community I want is all in this neighbourhood.

A good memory I have of my neighbourhood happened about two years ago. I and my pal were playing games and we were drinking so many energy drink we were HYPED! So we started walking down the road to Britannia and decided to climb it. When we got to the top there was the most beautiful sight; the stars and the city made the best picture I have ever seen. Such a beautiful neighbourhood; such a beautiful city.

DUSTIN

GRANDVIEW WOODLAND IS AWESOME BECAUSE...

Until the end of the Second World War, horses were still commonly used to deliver coal, ice and food throughout Grandview Woodland. Neighbourhood children would often feed the horses.

Ten Years Later

When I was six years old my parents moved our family to Vancouver B.C. We have been living here happily for 10 years now. I have been keeping my culture by coming to UNYA (Urban Native Youth Association) and every once and awhile I go to the women's drum group. I come to UNYA because they keep me grounded here. They make sure I have a safe place to go and I am not wandering the streets. My parents know where I am when I am here; they also know what I am doing here.

Okay, this year my parents decided it was time for some of us to go to Bella Bella for a vacation and I decided I wanted to go as well. My father, Patrick Sr., went up a week before us; his family was paying his way up. One week later, my mother Genevieve, brother Patrick Jr., and I went up north. We were all sad because my older sister Mabel wasn't able to come up because she had school. On the last ferry to Bella Bella I couldn't stop laughing because everyone was asking why I had a feeling I wasn't going to be able to survive on a reservation. On the reserve I wouldn't be able to do most of the things I like to do. Quite a bit of my family started crying because they thought I was too urbanized to even go up.

I was up there for an entire week. I had people calling me Mabel, my sister's name, until my mom finally decided to correct them. My mom showed me who my cousins were; even the older ones were what I would call little kids.

The most exciting part of my vacation was going on the boat. When I was little that was all I would love to do. To me, I believed the sea was somewhere I needed to be. The only reason I went on the boat this time was because we needed money to pay for our trip back to our home in North Vancouver. The bank machines in Bella Bella were empty every time we tried to get money out so we ended up going to Shearwater. Shearwater was a big part of my life when I was little too. That's where we would go for our birthdays and that is also where we would go to play in a bigger park.

The main reason we went to Bella Bella was for my nanny's potlatch. During the potlatch we did some adoptions, reaffirming of names and giving names, coming of age, family dancing, uplifting of the babies and then traditional dancing. Everyone who was at the potlatch was proud of me because I got up and did our traditional dancing. They were surprised to find out that it was my first time in six years and I was dancing like I have been dancing my entire life. At the end of the potlatch they gave things away. My nanny was happy because she was finally able to throw the potlatch of her dreams, which was for everyone to eat with proper utensils instead of paper plates and plastic cutlery. She had us eating with glass bowls, plates and using steel cutlery.

The longer I was there, the more it seemed like I hadn't moved away at all. I started remembering everyone; it felt like I was there only for a couple days after all. It was nice to see my nanny considering she isn't doing so well. I am happy that she has wonderful people to take care of her. By the end of the week I didn't want to leave but, at the same time, it was way too expensive for us up there. I had missed my sister so when we got back I asked to be dropped off at home right away just so I could see her. I don't think I could ever live without my sister, at least not right now. I need her in my life. So the next trip we have planned is for the entire family to go together. I hope I will be going back up to Bella Bella soon.

JAYLEEN (SWEETHEART)

Experience, Strength and Hope

I grew up in a small town called Tsawwassen, where almost everyone was rich and Caucasian. I am Native, Japanese, Irish and Scottish. So, growing up as one of the few mixed people in a small town was difficult, especially because I didn't know anything about my native ancestry due to my mother being adopted. Even though I grew up in a loving and supportive family, I ended up hanging out with troubled kids and using drugs and alcohol by the time I was 12 years old.

Once I started using I couldn't stop. I would drink and use drugs every weekend and sometimes during the week. From the age of 13 I couldn't remember a whole night; just bits and pieces, usually during my first couple of drinks, then little snippets here and there. I felt like part of me was missing and like no one actually liked me so I was always trying to impress people. I ended up making some friends down on the Tsawwassen Nation Reserve. I felt at home there and like that missing piece of me had been found because they considered me family and would call me 'cuz'. Things started going downhill very fast; there was fighting, drama, police and lots of drugs and alcohol.

I stopped hanging out on the rez when I got a boyfriend. I would spend all of my time with him and we were drinking almost every day. It was July 2007 when my mom, sister and I moved to Vancouver and I started school at Total Education, an alternate school. I would bus out to Ladner to see my boyfriend during the week and every weekend to spend time with him and drink.

I went to school hungover one day and was sent to the head teacher because that's not allowed. I was going to be kicked out of school if I didn't see a drug and alcohol counsellor at least 4 times. So I started seeing her but I didn't feel that I needed extra help; I felt that I could handle it on my own. I tried to just have non-alcoholic beer, tried drinking a glass of water between each beer and sharing beers but they only worked once or twice. Then I went back to my crazy out of control drinking.

My A&D counsellor helped me get into a day treatment program called Watari. They are a harm reduction program that helps youth to cut down or stop altogether. They helped me find out what caused me to drink and helped me to communicate better with my family and boyfriend. They showed me how to have fun while sober by taking me out on field trips. I continued to drink and tried to control it but was still having difficulties staying in control.

About a month after leaving Watari, I was referred to a residential treatment centre called Peak House. I ended up going on a fishing trip with my boyfriend instead of showing up on the scheduled date. When we got back I decided I really needed to stop drinking. I called Peak House and they told me that I needed a week sober before entering the house so I called detox and got in immediately.

After a wonderful time at detox, I went to treatment in East Van at Peak House. It was a bit scary at first but then I made friends and we had a great time. We had different types of group sessions throughout the week as well as outings. It was Peak House that introduced me to

Alcoholics Anonymous and Narcotics Anonymous. I was able to get to know my sister again and rebuild the broken relationship with her, my mom and my dad. I had a freaking awesome time there with my new friends, getting to know myself and actually being happy in my own skin. I was able to learn about smudging and the different traditions. I almost left about halfway through the program but remembering my sister and our new relationship helped me stay the whole 10 weeks. I commenced from Peak House on August 11th, 2008.

I continued going to AA and some NA meetings; I got a sponsor to help me through the tough times and to walk me through the 12 steps to a happy sober life. Most of my crew mates went back out using but one stayed sober and helped me to stay in AA and live a sober life. At 9 months of sobriety I stopped going to meetings and then, on the date of my 10 months, March 27th 2009, I went to my boyfriend's and drank. I didn't stop drinking for another 10 months.

During my relapse I continued to tell everyone I was sober. I started school at the Native Education College taking the Family & Community Counselling Program. Due to my drinking I was getting bad grades and missing school. I lost everything that I had gained and more.

In December 2009, my friend from Peak House asked me to come to an AA meeting where he was going to be the featured speaker because he wanted support. In order to keep up the image that I was still sober, I went. Sitting in that meeting and hearing him share, it reminded me of how happy I was in sobriety and of how happy I could be again. When the meeting was over, we went outside and I broke down crying. I was so appreciative of him inviting me and bringing me back to Alcoholics Anonymous. I drank a couple of more times after that and decided that I was done. I realized that I would have to leave my boyfriend in order to be able to focus on myself and my sobriety. I started going to meetings, making sober friends and got a new sponsor.

I started volunteering again and I graduated from NEC with my Counselling Certificate. I was able to really connect with my Native and Japanese ancestry and I have been exploring all areas of these cultures.

I enjoy the dancing, food and culture at the Friendship Centre and all of the wonderful, loving people that welcome you into their lives. For three years, since the summer of 2009, I have done the Pulling Together Canoe Journey with UNYA along with other exciting things to add to my adventures. My first canoe journey was during my relapse but I stayed sober for the whole time of the journey out of respect for the canoe and my canoe family.

I am now 21 years old with almost 20 months of sobriety and I have gotten back everything I lost and more. I now have my family, friends that truly care about me, the ability to help other alcoholics and addicts, and a happiness in my gut that will never go away as long as I am sober. I will be getting more education so that I can work at Peak House, Watari and UNYA. I want to help youth get the life that I have. I have the best family ever and that includes my AA family. I have been happy and sober since January 2nd, 2011 and looking forward to many more years of good sobriety. But I must remember to take things one day at a time.

You & Me

I love The Drive. My home for four years. But it's the people who make Grandview Woodland a wonderful place to live.

So much to do and see and learn and share and hear and say
So little few the hours, minutes, seconds in a day
Where and how do we begin with what and when and who
Of all the possibilities, I'm glad that I met you!

Let's explore this life
Smell the flowers, taste the spice
Come ease away complexity
Indulge unrushed simplicity, you & me.

Tensions, doubts & expectations, conflicts, hurts & fears
Spring up any second deeply rooted over years
Games & double messages & battles of the will
Words make easy weapons; yes can pierce and looks do kill!

No! Let's explore this life
Smell the flowers, taste the spice
Come ease away anxiety
Indulge in rich simplicity, you & me.

Status, customs, fads, peer pressures: the car, the look, the drink
Everyone is doing it! What will the neighbors think?
Keep up with the Jones, but don't rock the status quo.
You can't do it your own way. We'll tell you where to go!

No! Let's explore this life
Smell the flowers, taste the spice
Come ease away conformity
Indulge in posh simplicity, you & me
You & Me!

CHERRYSE KAISER

newSTART

newSTART, located at 1691 East Pender Street, is a community-based 13 week employment bridging program for women who are dealing with violence and abuse issues and currently on income assistance. Operating for the past 10 years, newSTART is funded by the Ministry of Housing and Social development (MHSD) and sponsored and administered by the Vancouver Eastside Educational Enrichment Society (VEEES). VEEES is a non-profit organization operating employment and educational programs in East Vancouver for over 22 years.

newSTART offers career exploration, job search skills training, an introduction to computers and computer skills, educational upgrading (GED), self-management workshops and identification replacement. The program also provides a three week work experience placement, a monthly transit pas and daycare top-up. Participants are encouraged to obtain certificates in self-defence as well as work related certificates for SuperHost and WorkSafe First Aid Level 1.

In addition to employment-related workshops, such as WHMIS, FOODSAFE, Criminal Record Checks (CPIC) and pardon assistance (CPIC), newSTART also provides opportunity for free clothing and financial support to meet employment and educational needs.

Participants also have the time and opportunity to deal with family custody issues, legal issues, and health concerns that may be preventing them from moving forward.

One-on-one counselling provides the opportunity for staff and participants to develop individualized needs assessments, access community resources and develop a personal action plan and determine educational needs.

As a part of our continuing commitment to program participants, newSTART offers past participants access to a variety of free services such as job search counselling, resume development, computer and internet access, and phone, local fax, message centre, and photocopy access. Other resources include employment/education resources as well as a job board, access to employment ads, employment postings and online job searches.

GRANDVIEW WOODLAND IS AWESOME BECAUSE...

You can be crazy since there is always someone crazier. It makes my job more interesting,
(Anonymous Barista)

A Crop of Kindness

The first spring we lived on Woodland Drive, we started a garden. We live in the basement apartment of a house and there is no yard to speak of, so we appropriated a section of grass between our fence and the sidewalk. I had never had my own garden before, but had grown up with an extensive vegetable garden tended lovingly by my parents. Feeling like a willing rookie, I launched into the happy experiment, imagining that we would enjoy an occasional morsel of fresh produce, and hoping the kids would gain an appreciation of where food comes from. What I had not bargained for was that this garden would become our personal ticket to meeting every friendly neighbour within walking distance of our home.

The kids and I dug up the grass. Our neighbours across the street asked if they could have the grass clods to fill in a corner of their own yard. We dug out a garden bed. An elderly man gave us tips on how to dig so as to go easy on our backs. We prepared the soil. A young man stopped his fancy car and, rolling down his window, offered us spare topsoil he had sitting in the alley just around the corner. Italian men from a nearby apartment building brought us offerings of the 'best' bean seeds and the 'tallest' kale, demonstrating with fingers how to plant them when English words failed them. Sometimes we came home to a pot of herbs or a flowering plant left for us. Neighbours offered us shade-loving ferns, oxalis and periwinkle to green up a narrow strip of dirt inside our fence, and they brought us basil, raspberries, and garlic chives for the sunny beds by the sidewalk.

We also planted sunflowers and zucchini and peas, watering them faithfully when the weather was dry. The upstairs neighbour offered us use of her hose whenever we needed it. The seeds sprouted and stretched. A little boy from down the street came to watch, fascinated. We weeded our small patch sparingly, unsure of what to pull out and what to leave in. Our next-door neighbour advised us on which were the weeds, and introduced her four big dogs to our two small children. Summer came, and with its warmth we weeded and watered and watched our garden grow. Meanwhile, just like the plants, we were putting down roots in our community.

Three years later, our garden has flourished and expanded to include multiple vegetable beds along with places for flowers, herbs, and shrubs, and a generous sandbox for the kids. Our connection to the community has grown right along with the garden plot.

The neighbours who took the grass clods bring us their empty jars so we can use them for canning. Their son comes to our house for play dates. The men who brought me their favourite seeds watch the garden grow as if it were theirs too, which it is. The little boy down the street came to plant seeds with us the next year, and he has subsequently become a favourite friend of our son and daughter.

Others share out muffins or mandarins as they pass by on their way home from getting groceries. One old gentleman, well-known by the neighbourhood children for carrying a pocketful of candy about with him, worried about us when we were out of town for an extended period, even enquiring after us with another neighbour. We were welcomed home by a present he had hung on our doorknob: rubber ducky toys from his grandchildren or a 'bag of chickens' as he described them. And the kind neighbour who helped identify our weeds from our vegetables? She is a daily visitor now for cups of tea and shared meals; our children like to walk her dogs or go to her house for a visit and toast, and twice weekly she comes to read the kids their bedtime stories. (Our youngest adores her.)

What a yield we have grown!

ANIKA KING

Photo courtesy of Kelley Montgomery

Playing Guitar

Moving to Vancouver from New Westminster wasn't easy. I didn't like the area, I didn't like the people, and to be honest, I was just being a brat so my mom would consider moving back to New West. I live pretty close to Commercial Drive, so my mother and I were going to get something from Tim Horton's. I was walking along when I walked by two men playing guitar together. One was much older, with a short but thick greying beard. The other man was in his late 20's. The older man was teaching the younger man a song. It was clear the younger man was struggling but the older man was so gentle and patient with him. It warmed my heart to see such kindness and I couldn't help but smile once I saw this. Seeing that man teach the younger man how to play guitar changed my opinion of the neighbourhood. I have met and seen many nice people since moving to this area of Vancouver, and I wouldn't want to live anywhere else.

AMANDA LUCAS

COMMERCIAL DRIVE

the landing pad of the rainbow family
a strip of peace in an otherwise hectic
plot of the garden that grows
those flowers that reach your hair
so fair so fair.
 (James)

Rhythm of the Drive

I just bought some batteries for this, my hand-held recorder. I'm gonna just walk down 'The Drive' now and see what comes to my senses. It is a beautiful day. Beautiful, beautiful, could walk forever in the sun I think.

Walking

Coming up to the organics store. A pretty girl I work with at the theater works there. I'm uh, kinda trepidatious about peering into the window–like a stalker or something.

"Smiling people pass by". I wonder if I said that too loud—they didn't turn around though. Guy sitting on the bench with earphones. Don't know if he heard me say hello but I won't let it get to me.

Sound of the traffic brings me back. Kids pass by—perfect.

Here we are at the organics store. I am gonna peer in now. Couldn't see her. A fellow asks me to buy some cherries.

Man it's hot. Cigarette in my hand as I walk. Careful not to blow smoke on anybody. I hear that in New York, Times Square, they are banning smoking. That sucks. I have been smoking for around 12 years now. I haven't even really thought about giving it up. See what happens, I guess.

Approaching Grandview Park. Where they have, uh, redone a lot of it. I guess it's good, though there is more concrete now. Doesn't quite seem as homey, if a park can be homey.

Walking, walking, walking. Once I actually forgot how to walk. That was kinda strange. I was really self-conscious. I don't know if I was all that cool.

Gonna puff my smoke here. Hang on. Mmm, my cigarette went out. Just a second, here, and I will relight it. (Click, click, click click).......done. I'm starting to huff and puff a little bit.

Couple with a dog pass by .Couples pass by talking. They are not holding hands. Maybe they are just friends. I don't care all that much.

In the shade now, much nicer. Passing by Highlife Records where I buy concert tickets. Last person I saw was Daniel Johnston at the Rio, it was pretty cool.

Passing the Italian cafes. The Italians sittin' out smoking even know there are laws and regulations (censored).

Co-Op bookstore: where they sold my book of poems. I decided not to sell them there anymore because they take too much of the profit.

Have a puff of my smoke here, Hang on......

I can't believe it cost me 5 dollars 50 for the batteries for this thing. What a rip-off. The guy gave me a bit of a deal though-it was actually $5.59. All I had was $5.50 so he spotted me 9 cents. Nice of him.

Dog. Dog looks vicious.

Walking

Somebody yelling on the other side of the street. F-this. F-that. I don't know if I approve of that word. I guess I don't like it .Seems to be some people's entire vocabulary is that word.

8 MINUTES NOW—about halfway there. Liquor store is on my left. I go in there every once and a while to be sure. Pick up some beer.

Feeling a bit self-conscious about doing this. Another puff of a smoke. Hang on a sec.

Two kids in a little wagon.

Chicken Burger for lunch. Only cost me a buck at the Kettle. Couldn't eat it all. I can't eat much in the mornings for some reason. How's that for interesting? At Tim Horton's now...Dairy Queen right –on—my—what was a Dairy Queen . They folded. Didn't do too well on the Drive.

There is a guy on the corner selling the Megaphone. A motorbike going by. I think one day, I might be riding a motorbike. Might as well. Gotta take some risks I guess, eh?

Alright, there is another smoker. Bless him.

Flight Centre on my right. Heading to Paris in about twenty days. More than excited. Planning it for about 5 months now. I don't know much French though—kinda worries me a bit.

Walking

Smoke starting to burn my fingers. Means that it is time to throw it out. At one time I would put the smoke out on the sidewalk or whatever and throw the butt in the garbage. Now I don't care that much and I don't know why that is.

Just passed an acquaintance. He lives in the same building as me.

Belgian Fries on my right. Wonderful fries, heart-attack-mayonnaise dip.

Just on the side of the, on the side of the, street. By the auto-body shop. A ton of books. I have a ton of books at home that I have just started and, uh, I haven't read too much of it.

Nice breeze. 13 MINUTES INTO THIS. Two thirds of the way home. All is well. Not sweating—which is good.

Guy passing by with a guitar, Strum, strum , strum it away man. I think about music.—am I getting too old? I don't know. Daniel Johnston.

Walking

Alright. JJ Bean is on my left now. I used to go there with a friend or two and have coffee Monday night but I haven't been for a while. I don't know why. Maybe it's because you can't smoke outside anymore.

Kids passing by on my right. A guy with a bowling ball passes me on my left.

I have another 5 blocks to home. I don't know how this is going to go on paper or, uh, on the computer. Too bad I can't just plug it in. I can't do that.

16 MINUTES IN. Nothing has really changed. Sun is still wonderful. Debating whether I should go to Safeway or should take this all the way home and have a recording of me from the Kettle Friendship Society to Friendship Court—where I live.

I'm gonna jaywalk. People selling on the side of the street. I don't have a nickel on me. Probably wouldn't buy anything anyways—saving for Paris, right?

(cough, cough) smokers cough.

Almost home. Turning the corner. Well I don't know what to say—about my experiment. It'll be a task, transcribing all of this. Almost home.

20 MINUTES IN MY LIFE. A walk that I have done thousands of times. Here I am. Passing under the sign "Friendship Court". 10, 9, 8, 7, 6, 5, 4, 3,2. –up the stairs. I am on the second floor. Finally, home

Quantum Physics

It seems like 65 years, not six and a half, since I moved to 'The Drive'. On January 20th, 2010 something happened to me which I would like to share. I was walking through Grandview Park. I did this habitually, cutting diagonally through the park to the back lane heading north. I must have done this a hundred times, but this time was different. I walked by a restaurant where a woman I barely knew was sweeping outside. A pleasant person, I nevertheless had no especially strong feelings towards her. But, this one time...

My understanding of quantum physics is sketchy to say the least but one of the arguable precepts is that there is at least one other dimension that exists along with the one we inhabit. Here time and space do not follow the same Newtonian principles that we take for granted. For the briefest of moments, watching this woman sweep dirt from the paved road was the most beautiful thing I had ever seen and I know I will ever see.

It wasn't about her looks, I couldn't see her face and her winter clothing obstructed her figure. Something about the motion of her sweeping, its rhythm and grace, exploded into my conscious and rendered me speechless. She continued to sweep and I walked by her, making sure she didn't see me.

After this, in the ensuing months, I began to see things - not dead people, mind you - but 'things' that I hadn't noticed before. Case in point, that spring, I was at a bus stop. The light from a rainbow that painted part of the sky that day shone through the plexiglass ceiling of the bus stop. It refracted onto the ground into a clipped rectangular rainbow of straight horizontal parallel lines. I exclaimed to the people waiting, "Look isn't that wonderful?" A woman said "Yes, isn't that nice?!"

Later in the summertime, I was at Broadway station. I jumped into a lineup for blueberries. I turned to a young man next to me. "Oh, did I take your place in line?" I asked. He didn't turn to look at me. "It doesn't matter" he said. I noticed he had fresh scratch marks on his neck and cheek and they looked painful. Cutting to the chase, I found out he had only recently arrived from Medicine Hat, Alberta. He had paid a damage deposit and two months rent and then his landlord had beaten him up and kicked him out of the apartment. The police were powerless to do anything. I didn't take pity on him so much as I took empathy. He stashed his belongings at my place and stayed elsewhere.

He loved the action of the city but he had had enough for the time being. Before I took him to the bus station, he showed me something on Youtube. A yogi or swami or whatever had a meditation technique which entailed mediating love towards a person. Intrigued, I did this off and on for a couple of days. When I awoke on August 20th something had happened. A knowing planted itself in my consciousness permanently that I would never imbibe alcohol ever again.

Since that morning, August 20th 2010, I haven't had a single moment when I've ever wanted to renege on my epiphany never to drink booze again. Not in the slightest. When someone offered me a drink, having no inkling of my metamorphosis, I forgot myself briefy but then, with the drink in front of me, I declined it emphatically.

In conclusion, I believe I had a brief glimpse of another dimension. More to the point, what I saw was the pinnacle, the best that this other world has to offer. On Commercial Drive a year and a half ago, I experienced unconditional love. At least, that's how I see it.

DAVID BERGER

Photo courtesy of Ella Mae Lansdowne

A Place of Acceptance

I have lived in East Vancouver for most of my life. While my husband was studying we lived for a few years in Toronto and then had a brief and somewhat traumatic exile in Richmond when we returned. But when we finally made it back to East Vancouver we settled in the Grandview Woodland neighbourhood and have felt relieved and "at home" ever since. This neighbourhood has taught me much about what it means to be a part of the human community.

In my efforts to become involved in the community I found myself volunteering at a community meal for marginalized people, sitting on the Grandview Woodland Drug & Alcohol Committee and the Vancouver Richmond Health Board Community Committee, teaching at Britannia High School and a few other odds and ends. It was through those experiences that my friendships with people who have found themselves on the margins of society grew.

In the winter of 2006 we moved into a home and opened it up to people who had, for many different reasons, found themselves on the street or in substandard housing. Together we shared meals, conversations, and frustrations around the lack of housing in the city. Together we shared involvement in activism during homeless action weeks, the Homes for All campaign, and the Olympics. Our work in the area of social change made sense with them involved.

I think the Grandview Woodland neighbourhood offers a place of acceptance for us all and I think it has been unique in the city in that respect. Many of the residents I know here are open minded and accepting of each other. I think especially of my neighbours during the time we had our house that was open to street folk. They were not too sure of us at first, but became good friends and advocates for living differently in the city. But there is also much resistance to living differently and at times I feel like we are losing the battle.

I wrote these two poems as reflections of my experience over the last few years. The first came after many conversations with people I had come to know in deeper ways and the second is a tribute to my friend Noah Sakee who died last October after a battle with cancer. These people are my inspiration to keep going in our struggle to become more fully human.

TERESA DIEWERT

How i see the world?

i see a world
of inequality and injustice
where lots have little
and little have lots.

i see a world
where people go after
all they can get
with no thought to how they
got what they've got
no thought
to the cost of what they've got.
no thought
to the gross injustice
of their privilege.

i see a world
in which those with lots
grasp for more;
an overflow of affluence.
a constant consumption
of nothing
that can give life.

i see a world
filled with distraction
distancing from
the other through unreal
reality tv
and the virtual reality
of video games
facebook and lavalife
What a life!
sitting in front of a computer
screen screaming for attention,
for someone to answer
a call for intimacy.

i also see a world
in which
many
have nowhere to lay their head to sleep
so
they creep
under my stairs.

i stare at them lying there
among the recycling and gardening tools,
the scraps of wood
wondering
if they see themselves
as scraps
of humanity.
they smile at me
tell me bits of their story.

i see a world
in which
many
are left to fend for themselves
after they have not behaved
they have been
discarded,
disregarded,
left on their own
at eight
or fifteen
or eighteen.
When is it the right age
to behave?
Children misbehave.
Who is responsible?

i see a world
in which
labels are applied
to smooth over
the complexities
of pain,
to smooth over
the confusion of grief,
to smooth over
the violence of abuse,
the reality of abandonment.

Labels:
alcoholic; addict; schizophrenic;
bipolar; FAS; ADHD; homeless; bum
If you ask me
these labels only
serve the labeler.

The labeled have no voice
in saying who they are.
they are reduced
by those with power
to something less than
the person they are

and
I find it hard not to see past the label
to the artist
stuck at 18
because that is where he knows his deepest rejection
or
stuck at 15
after he's lost count of foster parents
or stuck at 8
as he watches his father murder his mother by mistake,
i think,
in a drunken state, i think.
i don't know all the details – don't want the details.

This is already
too much
for me to see.

i see too much.

but, i believe

these two worlds
need to
see each other.

- TERESA DIEWERT

Noah's Memorial

There was so much
I didn't know about
Noah....
4 living sisters...
how he came to be here
rather than up North with them...

but that was Noah
not one for talking much about himself

there was silence
in the Noah I knew

he did not want to
divulge
too much to me...

What I will remember though
is his infectious laughter
and impish spirit,
his love of cooking

I will remember his dedication to
the cause of housing
in this place
expressed through
willingness to dig latrines
that looked like
they would bury him alive

I will remember his determination to be
at Olympic Tent Village
staying clear headed there
focused
in his quiet way
tidying the kitchen, serving food,
patrolling the perimeters
washing dishes with me at deyas

He wanted to be part of
a change.

His tiny body gave up
on his large spirit.

I will remember his stubbornness
expressed in his
love of food.
French fries on an empty stomach?

...or no stomach at all!

I will remember countless trips to
hospital emergency rooms

Doctors, thinking they knew you,
assumptions made
games played
by them and you
I think they wrote you off
did wrong by you, took too long
but
your stubbornness didn't help...

and I try to understand you
...not an easy thing to do
when your bath towels
were strewn all over the basement
and your life was disappearing before
my eyes
eyes that cry for you, Noah.

I remember thinking Noah knew he was not going to get better.
So he was going to get the better
of a system that had
taken so much from him -
family, culture, hope for a future.

Noah's Memorial Cont.

Noah taught me a lot
about my culture.
A culture with seemingly limited understanding
of the value of human lives
only measuring in money
deeply rooted in racism
fully practiced in patronizing policies
of removal.

You fought a good fight,
Noah.
And I consider it an honour
to have known you.

- TERESA DIEWERT

Stranger in the City

Hi, my name is Joan. I am Coast Salish and from Semiahmoo. I remember the first day I came to Vancouver. I was told that I was going to move in with my stepdad for a while. I had never been to Vancouver before so I thought it was going to be exactly like White Rock or Chilliwack. We were driving in an old minivan and had the radio blasting to the point where my ears were going to explode. My mom told me to be happy and excited; I didn't want to be, because I knew I wasn't going to see her for a while. As we entered Vancouver, the first thing I noticed was the tall buildings; they reminded me of the trees on my reserve but the buildings made me feel smaller and vulnerable. We made it to my stepdad's place, I didn't see him for a few years and I noticed he changed a bit, his hair was greyer and he looked happier. That same day he told us that we had to go shopping for groceries at Metrotown. I didn't know what Metrotown was, I thought it was some little village or store. He didn't have a car so we had to take the Skytrain. I thought, "That's silly, a train in the sky." When we got to the Skytrain my stepdad had to force me on to it and kept telling me that everything was going to be okay. I stepped on the train and thought, "I'm going to die." The train started moving and it scared me, I started to fall everywhere and almost fell on an elderly lady. I felt like if I fell on her she would shatter so I got shy and hid behind my stepdad. As the train stopped at Metrown I fell again, but instead I landed on this older man who didn't look too happy.

GRANDVIEW WOODLAND IS AWESOME BECAUSE…

…it's a friendly and open community. Rarely on my travels in either Europe or Canada have I seen such a close knit and yet diverse community.
(Ollie)

Watari

Watari is a small registered social profit organization with a volunteer Board of Directors. Our primary mission is to facilitate positive change in the lives of at-risk children, youth, their families and communities in the Downtown Eastside and the Greater Vancouver/Richmond areas.

Watari was registered as a charitable society in June 1986 as a small scale service offering individualized support services to high risk youth from mobile offices (cars). We then began operating out of Ray-Cam Community Centre in the Downtown Eastside of Vancouver in 1989. Watari now has two permanent locations in East Vancouver and operates 5 ongoing programs. Members of the community who access our services identify that substance misuse has been a problem in their own lives or in the lives of their families.

Watari was developed in 1986 in a response to a lack of services and programs for high-risk/street involved youth in Vancouver. Watari began to provide one-to-one youth care services to the Vancouver Intensive Child Care Resource (ICCR). ICCR offered services to extremely high-risk youth within an integrated case management approach. Watari was part of this multi disciplinary team comprised of two other agencies and five government ministries.

In 1989, Watari was invited to conduct an alcohol and drug needs assessment study in the Downtown East Side area of Vancouver. This was an extensive community collaboration that resulted in the establishment of the Youth and Family Alcohol and Drug Strategy. This was a non-traditional approach to alcohol and drug programs and counselling with a strong emphasis on community development and peer leadership training. An administrative community council comprised of residents guided the direction of the program.

In 1993-94, Watari established an administrative office in the Downtown Eastside area of Vancouver. In 1993 a study called Community Organization Strategy for At Risk Youth in the Downtown Eastside/Strathcona Area was written and published. Peerworks - Substance Abuse Training for youth peer helpers was written and published by Watari. Watari developed and implemented a Caregiver Training Curriculum. Participants in the training were employed for one-to-one services, residential detox, peer support and outreach services.

In 1996, Watari administered a community-based initiative designed to develop protection strategies for street involved children and youth at risk of sexual exploitation. The project was called The Child and Youth Protection Strategy.

In 1997, Watari partnered with Douglas College, Faculty of Child, Family and Community Services to develop the Working with Street Involved Youth Training Program. A Mental Health Specialty was added to the training in 1999 for the third session.

In 1998, the lack of post detox transitional supports for youth prompted Watari to shift from detox services to the creation of the Street Youth Day Treatment Program. The Youth and Family Alcohol and Drug Services expanded services in an initiative called the Downtown Eastside HIV Strategy.

In 2000, the Street Youth Day Treatment Program Follow-up Study was completed. Also, the ICCR was disbanded and replaced by the Specialized Youth Response Program (SYRP) in a partnership with another agency.

In 2001, Watari entered into the process of accreditation with The Rehabilitation Accreditation Commission (CARF).

In 2004, Watari began the SRO Building Managers Program. This program includes an education series that is made available to professionals, volunteers and community members – addressing issues such as dual diagnosis, conflict resolution and accessing appropriate services. Watari also partnered with Hollyburn Family

Services, Elizabeth Frye Society and Capilano Services Society to provide a full continuum of services to youth and families on the North Shore. Watari developed the youth transitioning to adulthood portfolio as well as a mentoring program for high risk youth, including community-based training models.

In 2006, our twentieth year in service, Watari was the successful proponent in a Request for Proposals with Vancouver Coastal Health to deliver a supported independent living program, TTIP, Transitioning to Independence Project. This program will support 20 young people, at different places along the addiction continuum, in maintaining housing and their goals around their own use.

Watari proudly took on the delivery of Hard Target Coordination in 2006 which had been developed in the community over the last decade. The program is well suited for the agency as the focus is on creating integrated case management approaches to work effectively with street-involved and hard to reach youth.

2008 welcomed the 8th edition of the Survival Manual! In addition to a new and vibrant image on the cover; funding from Social Planning and Research Council of BC allowed Watari to create a web-based version of the manual with its own interactive website : www.survivalmanual.org.

In 2009, The Transitioning to Independence Project (TTIP) was expanded to support homeless pregnant or parenting youth. The through funding from the Vancouver Foundation will allow up to 25 youth to be housed in market housing over the three years of its funding. Evaluation will include the existing TTIP program.

And the story continues...

This is what community means to people at Watari

SECURITY MITLIED VULNERABLE INNOVATIVE AUTHENTIC BELONGING TOGETHER SUPPORTING SIEMPRE FREE INCLUSION PARTNERSHIP LOVING AJUDAR CREATIVITY PERDONAR WATARI CUIDADO FORCA GOOD MACHT APRENDER COMMUNICATION COMMUNITY COOPERATIVE DIVINE HEALTHY CONNECTING UNIDAD HELPING PROMESSA FEELING PODER DIVERSITY SAFETY HAPPY MEANS HYHY SENCE LIVE DAJE

Glen Caponero and the Black Dog

Most people in the Grandview area are familiar with Figaro's Garden, an astoundingly beautiful garden centre at Victoria and East Third Avenue, that my beloved husband, Glen Caponero, built over a decade. But only some know that Glen took his own life on 25 August 2011. He was 45 years old, and we were just 10 days shy of our first year wedding anniversary. Suicide always brings us face to face with something raw and brutal and painful, and as a society we recoil and prefer not to talk about it. But this reaction, while understandable, is a terrible mistake. We need to talk about suicide, so that those who survive it know they are neither alone nor at fault; but perhaps more importantly so that those who are contemplating it understand that they will devastate everyone they love, and that there is an alternative salvation from their pain, if only they reach out. So here is Glen's and my story.

Glen and I met three years ago, when I came back to Vancouver to care for my mother after she developed breast cancer. I wasn't planning on staying, and Glen wasn't looking for anything serious, having recently ended a 19-year relationship. We enjoyed a rare 'no expectations' situation, in which we simply got to know one another. Glen asked me many times why I fell in love with him so quickly, and I joked that it was because he had a great apartment, a fantastic wardrobe which fit me perfectly, and Bruno, undoubtedly the most adorable dog on the planet. But the truth was more profound: he was The One. Since the beginning, we did not spend a single night apart, and we worked together 24/7 too, first in Figaro's Garden, and for the last two years at our farm here on Galiano Island.

Our presence on Galiano was entirely random. Glen took me here for a luxury spa weekend one August - typical of his generosity even when he himself didn't have a penny - and one afternoon when it was too cold to go to the beach but too fine to stay indoors we decided to go for a bike ride. We aimed for one of the island's many parks, but we never made it. Instead, we stopped at an abandoned wooden house on a sunny slope with an overgrown grassy driveway. Somehow, it called us in for a peek. Because we were bored and too tired to cycle further, we rang the estate agent, and a few weeks later we were, to our shock and delight, the owners of a dauntingly huge project and dream. For two years we worked like slaves to turn our 10 acres into a haven, and by the day of Glen's death we had largely succeeded, though I know Glen always felt a lot of pressure to do still more. His bubblingly creative mind fired ideas out like popcorn, and he then worked harder than anyone I have ever known to turn them into reality. I remain in awe of everything that Glen could do. The results are all around our house and farm, and despite what happened here it remains for me a place of profound peace and beauty. Someone sent me a sympathy card which said "Some people bring so great a light to the world that even after they are gone, the light remains". Glen's light is everywhere at Figaro's Garden and here at 617 Bluff Road.

I don't really know why the cunning and evil black dog finally got Glen that afternoon. Probably a perfect firestorm of factors: burn-out from overwork, financial pressures, a questionable prescription medication that has been associated with higher suicide risks, deep-rooted scars from an abusive childhood, and also – to my eternal regret - a vicious argument with me. But that morning we had happily discussed getting a new dog, and Glen was excited about the imminent arrival of a new breed of chicken that he had ordered. That afternoon we were to go to the beach, but instead we had a heated argument over something trivial, and I went for a nap. When I woke up Glen was gone and instead there was simply his body, hanging from a rope in our giant maple tree. He was the man I kissed 10,000 frogs to find, the man who landed me gently down in BC, my birthplace, after 27 years of living in different countries abroad, the man I looked forward to growing old with.

He could be gnarly sometimes, but in truth Glen was the most loveable of men - kind, honest, handsome, generous, sensual, intelligent, capable, adventurous, compassionate, funny, and gentle. He cried when a sick baby chick that we had hatched from an egg died. He would buy me presents, out of the blue, just because. He was the rock anyone could rely on in a crisis. There was truly something divine about him; everyone who met him just wanted to be in his presence and to be loved by him. But when the black dog managed to get Glen's ear it convinced him he was despicable and unlovable. In his suicide note, he said he was sorry, but he was disgusted and disappointed in himself, and he could no longer stand the pain of not being the man he was supposed to be. It was a moment of triumph for the black dog with a lifetime of consequence for me, and everyone who knew and loved Glen. His suicide is a pain that we will carry with us always. Our challenge is to remember not the body hanging from the tree, but instead to remember the real Glen - the most lovable of men, with his billion kilowatt smile of happiness.

PETER WORTHINGTON

Photo courtesy of Brian Collins